Southern
CAST IRON

Southern

CAST IRON

Heirloom Recipes for Your Favorite Skillets

hm | books

hm | books

EXECUTIVE VICE PRESIDENT/CCO Brian Hart Hoffman
VICE PRESIDENT/EDITORIAL Cindy Smith Cooper
ART DIRECTOR Cailyn Haynes

TASTE OF THE SOUTH EDITORIAL

EDITOR Brooke Michael Bell
CREATIVE DIRECTOR/PHOTOGRAPHY Mac Jamieson
ASSOCIATE EDITOR Josh Miller
ASSISTANT EDITOR Avery Driggers
EDITORIAL ASSISTANT Alexa Bode
COPY EDITOR Maria Parker Hopkins
CONTRIBUTING COPY EDITOR Donna Baldone
STYLISTS Amy Hannum, Anna Pollock Rayner
CONTRIBUTING STYLIST Malinda Kay Nichols
SENIOR PHOTOGRAPHERS John O'Hagan, Marcy Black Simpson
PHOTOGRAPHERS Sarah Arrington, William Dickey, Stephanie Welbourne, Kamin Williams
CONTRIBUTING PHOTOGRAPHER Kimberly Finkel Davis
TEST KITCHEN DIRECTOR Janice Ritter
EXECUTIVE CHEF Rebecca Treadwell
TEST KITCHEN PROFESSIONALS Allene Arnold, Melissa L. Brinley, Kathleen Kanen, Janet Lambert, Aimee Bishop Lindsey, Anna Theoktisto, Loren Wood
CONTRIBUTING TEST KITCHEN PROFESSIONALS Rachael Daylong, Virginia Hornbuckle, Chantel Lambeth
TEST KITCHEN ASSISTANT Anita Simpson Spain
SENIOR DIGITAL IMAGING SPECIALIST Delisa McDaniel
DIGITAL IMAGING SPECIALIST Clark Densmore
MULTIMEDIA DIRECTOR Bart Clayton
ONLINE MARKETING MANAGER Eric Bush
ONLINE EDITOR Victoria Phillips

hm
hoffmanmedia

PRESIDENT Phyllis Hoffman DePiano
EXECUTIVE VICE PRESIDENT/COO Eric W. Hoffman
EXECUTIVE VICE PRESIDENT/CCO Brian Hart Hoffman
EXECUTIVE VICE PRESIDENT/CFO G. Marc Neas
VICE PRESIDENT/FINANCE Michael Adams
VICE PRESIDENT/DIGITAL MEDIA Jon Adamson
VICE PRESIDENT/MANUFACTURING Greg Baugh
VICE PRESIDENT/EDITORIAL Cindy Smith Cooper
VICE PRESIDENT/CONSUMER MARKETING Silvia Rider
VICE PRESIDENT/ADMINISTRATION Lynn Lee Terry

Hoffman Media
1900 International Park Drive, Suite 50
Birmingham, Alabama 35243
hoffmanmedia.com

ISBN # 978-1-940772-07-3

Printed in Mexico

Cover recipes on pages 134, 141, 158
Photography by Marcy Black Simpson/Photo Styling by Anna Pollock Rayner

Contents

INTRODUCTION

Cast iron might be the most sacred of all Southern cookware, but cooks around the world have been preparing their most cherished recipes in it for centuries.

PASSED DOWN THROUGH GENERATIONS, every pan, skillet, pone tray, and Dutch oven tells a story. Lacquered from years of suppers, the oldest cast-iron relics are blackened and bubbled from open-pit fires and hearth cooking. Heavy with history, each piece carries around glorious cooking traditions as readily as it sops up seasoning. Cooking cornbread, pork chops, and upside down cakes seasons skillets like nothing else can. Flavor seeps into cast iron's porous surface, making it the original nonstick pan, perfect for frying chicken and baking cakes.

Classic Southern cast-iron dishes nourish the body and feed the soul. There's simply no better way to brown, sear, roast, and caramelize. Cast iron's unrivaled ability to produce dry, even heat makes it a staple for time-honored recipes. But just like foodways that are forever evolving, so are the uses for cast iron. Deep-dish pizzas, stuffed peppers, and skillet cookies now join the spread. You'll find all of these recipes and many others on the pages of *Southern Cast Iron* to delight and devour for years to come.

CAST-IRON CARE

If you take the time and effort to properly care for your beloved cast-iron cookware, it will reward you and your family with generations of loyal service. Follow these tips to treat your heirlooms with tender, loving care.

RESPECT YOUR COOKWARE Taking care of your cast iron means understanding its likes and dislikes.

Likes
Cooking with oil
Dry cupboards
Gentle cleaning

Dislikes Water
Acidic foods
Soaps and harsh abrasives

CAST-IRON CLEANING: BEST PRACTICES
When it comes to cleaning cast iron, there is one commandment: Respect the finish. Hot water is the best tool, combined with gently scrubbing with a sponge or paper towel. Resist the urge to use soap, as it can affect the finish of your pan and the flavor of future dishes. Avoid immersing your cast-iron cookware in water, which increases the risk of rusting.

Scour Power If you're stuck with stubborn bits of cooked-on food, add about ¼ cup of kosher salt to the warm pan, and gently scour with a folded kitchen towel. Rinse, and dry thoroughly.

Clean Promptly Never put your cookware away dirty. Excess oil will pool and solidify, making future cleaning difficult. For best results, clean pots and pans immediately after cooking.

Drying Cast Iron After rinsing, it's crucial to dry your cookware completely. Wipe dry with a clean dish towel or paper towel, then apply a thin coat of oil, rubbing it into the surface. Heat on the stove over medium-low heat or in the oven at 300° for several minutes, or until dry.

CAST-IRON REVITALIZATION If your heirlooms fall victim to rust, don't despair. Follow these steps to get them back in action.

1. Scrub with a stiff-bristle brush and hot soapy water to remove any rust or buildup. Rinse well, and dry completely.
2. Brush a light coating of oil on inside and outside of pan.
3. Place a sheet of aluminum foil or a rimmed baking sheet on lower rack of oven to catch drips. Place oiled pan upside down on middle rack of oven.
4. Bake at 350° for approximately 1 hour. Turn off oven, and let pan cool in oven. Repeat as necessary. Store in a cool, dry place.

SEASONING TIP Be conservative when applying oil to your pans for seasoning. Using too much can result in a sticky residue.

NO HEIRLOOM? NO PROBLEM If you haven't been blessed with the gift of your grandma's beloved skillet, don't worry—preseasoned cast-iron pans are widely available. When using your preseasoned cast-iron pan for the first time, rinse with water, and dry completely. Before cooking, brush cookware lightly with oil, and heat slowly.

Supper

Chicken and Rice

YIELD: APPROXIMATELY 6 SERVINGS

1   **(3- to 4-pound) whole chicken, cut into pieces**
4   **teaspoons kosher salt, divided**
1½ **teaspoons ground black pepper, divided**
2   **tablespoons extra-virgin olive oil**
1   **medium onion, chopped**
1   **green bell pepper, chopped**
6   **cloves garlic, minced**
3   **medium tomatoes, chopped**
1   **tablespoon dried oregano**
1   **teaspoon ground cumin**
1½ **cups basmati rice, rinsed**
1   **cup dry white wine**
1½ **cups water**
1   **teaspoon hot sauce**
1   **cup frozen peas**
½   **cup pimiento-stuffed green olives**

Season chicken with 2 teaspoons salt and 1 teaspoon pepper. In a large cast-iron skillet, heat olive oil over high heat. Working in batches, cook chicken until browned on both sides, approximately 6 minutes per side. Remove chicken from skillet, and set aside. Reduce heat to medium.

Add onion and bell pepper to skillet. Cook, stirring occasionally, until tender, approximately 5 minutes. Stir in garlic, tomatoes, oregano, and cumin. Cook until almost all liquid has evaporated, approximately 10 minutes.

Stir in rice, wine, 1½ cups water, hot sauce, remaining 2 teaspoons salt, and ½ teaspoon pepper. Return chicken to skillet; stir in frozen peas and olives. Bring to a boil, and immediately reduce heat to medium-low. Cover, and cook until rice is tender and chicken is cooked through, approximately 30 minutes.

Shrimp Étouffée

YIELD: APPROXIMATELY 4 SERVINGS

¼   cup vegetable oil
⅓   cup all-purpose flour
½   cup chopped celery
½   cup chopped onion
½   cup chopped green bell pepper
1½   teaspoons Cajun seasoning
     or to taste
½   teaspoon salt
4   bay leaves
1   large sprig fresh thyme
1   clove garlic, minced
2½   cups hot Shrimp Stock
     (recipe follows)
2   pounds large fresh shrimp, peeled
     and deveined (tails left on), shells
     reserved for Shrimp Stock
½   cup chopped seeded tomato
Hot cooked rice
Garnish: chopped green onion

SHRIMP STOCK
Reserved shrimp shells
3   cups water
½   lemon
4   sprigs fresh parsley
4   sprigs fresh thyme
½   small onion

FOR ÉTOUFFÉE: In a 10-inch cast-iron skillet, heat oil over medium heat; gradually stir in flour. Stir constantly with a wooden spoon until mixture is a deep caramel color, 15 to 20 minutes. Add celery, onion, and bell pepper; cook until vegetables begin to soften, approximately 5 minutes. Add Cajun seasoning, salt, bay leaves, thyme, and garlic; cook 1 minute.

Gradually add hot Shrimp Stock to skillet, stirring to combine. Bring to a boil. Reduce heat to medium-low, and simmer, stirring frequently, until mixture is smooth and thickened, approximately 20 minutes. Add shrimp and tomato. Cover, and cook until shrimp are pink and firm, approximately 7 minutes. (Discard bay leaves and thyme sprig before serving.) Serve with rice, and garnish with green onion, if desired.

FOR SHRIMP STOCK: In a large saucepan, combine shrimp shells, 3 cups water, lemon, parsley, thyme, and onion; bring to a boil. Reduce heat to medium-low; simmer 30 minutes. Strain stock through a fine-mesh sieve into a medium bowl. Discard solids. Add additional water, if needed, to yield 2½ cups stock.

Old-Fashioned Chicken Pot Pie

YIELD: APPROXIMATELY 6 SERVINGS

4   tablespoons butter

1   cup chopped celery

1   cup finely chopped carrot

½   cup chopped green onion

½   cup all-purpose flour

3   cups chicken broth

1   cup whole milk

2   teaspoons salt

1   teaspoon ground black pepper

1½   cups peeled and chopped Yukon gold potato

3   cups shredded cooked chicken

½   cup frozen cut green beans, thawed

½   cup frozen petite peas, thawed

½   (14.1-ounce) package refrigerated piecrusts (1 sheet)

2   tablespoons heavy whipping cream

Preheat oven to 425°.

In a 12-inch cast-iron skillet, melt butter over medium heat. Add celery, carrot, and green onion. Cook, stirring frequently, 4 to 5 minutes. Sift flour over vegetables, stirring well. Cook, stirring frequently, until flour begins to thicken and brown slightly, 2 to 3 minutes. Gradually add broth, stirring well to remove any lumps. Cook, stirring frequently, until thickened, 5 to 7 minutes. Add milk, salt, and pepper, stirring well. Add potato, and cook 6 to 8 minutes, stirring frequently.

Remove from heat. Add chicken, green beans, and peas to skillet, stirring to combine.

Unroll piecrust, and place over filling in skillet. Crimp edges as desired. With a sharp knife, make 4 (1½-inch) vents in center of dough. Brush with cream.

Bake until crust is golden brown, 15 to 20 minutes.

Steak Fajitas

YIELD: APPROXIMATELY 8 SERVINGS

2   **pounds skirt steak, thinly sliced against the grain**

1   **(12-ounce) bottle Mexican beer, such as Corona**

2   **limes, juiced**

4   **cloves garlic, minced**

4   **teaspoons salt, divided**

2   **teaspoons ground black pepper**

½   **teaspoon ground red pepper, optional**

1   **medium yellow or orange bell pepper, sliced**

1   **medium red bell pepper, sliced**

2   **jalapeño peppers, seeded and sliced**

1   **medium red onion, sliced**

1   **medium yellow onion, sliced**

12   **corn tortillas, warmed**

Avocado slices

Fresh cilantro

Salsa

In a large bowl, combine beef, beer, lime juice, garlic, 2 teaspoons salt, black pepper, and red pepper, if using. Cover, and refrigerate 20 minutes.

Heat a large cast-iron grill pan over high heat until very hot. Spray pan with nonstick cooking spray, and add bell pepper, jalapeño, and 1 teaspoon salt. Cook until tender, approximately 4 minutes. Remove from pan. Set aside, and keep warm.

Add onion and remaining 1 teaspoon salt to grill pan. Cook until browned and translucent, approximately 3 minutes. Remove from pan. Set aside, and keep warm.

Remove steak from marinade; pat dry. Discard marinade. Spray grill pan with nonstick cooking spray. Cook steak in batches over high heat, stirring occasionally, until very browned and slightly crisp, approximately 4 minutes per batch. Serve in tortillas with peppers, onions, avocado, cilantro, and salsa.

Southern-Fried Catfish

YIELD: APPROXIMATELY 8 SERVINGS

Vegetable oil, for frying

1½ cups whole buttermilk

2 cups plain white or yellow
  cornmeal

1 tablespoon salt

2 teaspoons garlic powder

2 teaspoons onion powder

1 teaspoon ground red pepper

8 (6-ounce) catfish fillets

In a large cast-iron Dutch oven, pour oil to halfway full. Heat oil over medium-high heat until a deep-fry thermometer reads 350°.

In a shallow bowl, pour buttermilk. In another shallow bowl, stir together cornmeal, salt, garlic powder, onion powder, and red pepper. Dip each catfish fillet in buttermilk, letting excess drain. Dredge each fillet in cornmeal mixture, shaking off excess.

Cook until golden brown, turning several times, 6 to 8 minutes. (Adjust heat as needed to maintain 350°.) Let drain on paper towels.

Chipotle-Caramelized Onion Meat Loaf

YIELD: APPROXIMATELY 6 SERVINGS

2   teaspoons canola oil
1½   cups chopped yellow onion
1½   teaspoons salt, divided
3   to 5 tablespoons water
2   slices soft white bread, torn
¼   cup whole milk
1   pound ground sirloin
1   pound ground pork
1   tablespoon chopped fresh thyme
1   tablespoon Worcestershire sauce
2   to 3 tablespoons chopped seeded
     chipotle chiles in adobo sauce
1   large egg
¾   cup shredded Monterey Jack
     cheese

Preheat oven to 350°.

In a medium skillet, heat canola oil over medium-high heat. Add onion; cook, stirring occasionally, until lightly browned around edges, approximately 4 minutes. Reduce heat to medium-low; add ¼ teaspoon salt, and slowly stir in 2 tablespoons water. Cook, stirring occasionally, until deep golden brown, approximately 10 minutes. (Stir in additional water, 1 tablespoon at a time, to prevent onion from sticking to pan, if needed.) Remove from heat. Set aside.

In a large bowl, combine bread and milk; let stand 5 minutes. Add beef, pork, remaining 1¼ teaspoons salt, thyme, Worcestershire, chiles, and egg, gently stirring until well combined. Gently press beef mixture into a 9x5-inch cast-iron loaf pan. Spread onion over beef mixture.

Bake until a meat thermometer inserted in center reads 160°, approximately 55 minutes. Remove from oven. Carefully tilt pan over a bowl to drain; discard drippings. Top meat loaf with cheese.

Bake until cheese melts, approximately 7 minutes. Let cool 15 minutes before serving.

Chicken-Fried Steak
with Milk Gravy

YIELD: APPROXIMATELY 6 SERVINGS

3/4 cup all-purpose flour, divided
1   tablespoon plus 2 teaspoons salt,
     divided
1   tablespoon plus 1 teaspoon
     ground black pepper, divided
1/2 teaspoon paprika
2   cups crushed saltine crackers
1   cup whole buttermilk
1   large egg
Vegetable oil, for frying
1 1/2 pounds cubed round steak, cut
     into 6 pieces
2   cups whole milk
Garnish: chopped fresh parsley,
     ground black pepper

In a shallow dish, combine 1/2 cup flour, 1 tablespoon salt, 1 tablespoon pepper, and paprika, whisking to combine.

In another shallow dish, combine 1 teaspoon salt, 1/2 teaspoon pepper, and saltines.

In a third shallow dish, whisk together buttermilk and egg.

In a deep cast-iron skillet or cast-iron Dutch oven, pour oil to a depth of 2 inches; heat over medium-high heat until a deep-fry thermometer reads 375°.

Working in batches, dredge steak pieces in flour, gently shaking off excess. Dip in egg mixture, letting excess drain. Coat steak pieces in cracker mixture, gently shaking off excess.

Add steak pieces to skillet, 2 at a time, and cook until golden brown and cooked through, 2 to 3 minutes per side. (Adjust heat as needed to maintain 375°.) Let drain on paper towels. Place in a single layer on a baking sheet, and place in a 200° oven to keep warm.

Drain oil, reserving 1/4 cup in skillet. Heat over medium heat. Add remaining 1/4 cup flour, whisking to combine. Cook until mixture thickens, 1 to 2 minutes. Gradually add milk, whisking until smooth. Add remaining 1 teaspoon salt and 1/2 teaspoon pepper to milk mixture. Cook, whisking constantly, until thickened, 4 to 5 minutes. Serve gravy over steaks. Garnish with parsley and pepper, if desired.

Stewed Okra with Chicken, Tomatoes, and Garbanzo Beans

YIELD: APPROXIMATELY 6 SERVINGS

4   **tablespoons extra-virgin olive oil, divided**

1½   **pounds boneless skinless chicken breasts**

1   **medium yellow onion, thinly sliced**

2   **cloves garlic, minced**

5   **cups chopped fresh okra**

1   **(28-ounce) can diced tomatoes**

½   **cup golden raisins**

2   **tablespoons fresh lemon juice**

1   **tablespoon curry powder**

2   **teaspoons sugar**

2   **teaspoons salt**

1   **(16-ounce) can garbanzo beans, drained and rinsed**

In a large cast-iron Dutch oven, heat 2 tablespoons olive oil over medium-high heat. Cook chicken until browned, 4 to 5 minutes per side. Remove chicken from pan, and set aside.

Add remaining 2 tablespoons olive oil to pan. Cook onion and garlic over medium heat until softened, 3 to 4 minutes. Return chicken to pan. Add okra and tomato; cover, and cook until chicken is cooked through, approximately 20 minutes. Add raisins, lemon juice, curry, sugar, and salt, stirring well. Cover, and cook 10 minutes.

Using two forks, shred chicken into large chunks. Stir in garbanzo beans, and cook until heated through.

Deep-Dish Pork and Collard Greens Pizza

YIELD: APPROXIMATELY 6 SERVINGS

CRUST

- ¾ **cup warm water (105° to 115°)**
- 1 **teaspoon active dry yeast**
- ½ **teaspoon sugar**
- ¼ **cup extra-virgin olive oil**
- 2¼ **cups all-purpose flour, divided**
- ¼ **cup plain white or yellow cornmeal**
- ½ **teaspoon salt**

FILLING

- 4 **teaspoons extra-virgin olive oil, divided**
- 1 **cup finely chopped onion**
- 1 **tablespoon minced fresh garlic**
- 1 **pound ground pork**
- 3 **cups chopped fresh collard greens**
- 2 **teaspoons fennel seed, crushed**
- ½ **teaspoon crushed red pepper**
- ⅓ **cup sun-dried tomatoes in oil, drained and chopped**
- 2 **teaspoons distilled white vinegar**
- 1⅓ **cups shredded smoked Cheddar cheese, divided**
- 2 **teaspoons plain white or yellow cornmeal**
- 1 **cup shredded whole milk mozzarella cheese**

FOR CRUST: In a large bowl, combine ¾ cup warm water, yeast, and sugar; let stand 5 minutes or until foamy. Add olive oil, 2 cups flour, cornmeal, and salt; stir until a soft dough forms.

Turn dough out onto a lightly floured surface. Knead until dough is smooth and elastic, approximately 6 minutes. (Add remaining ¼ cup flour, 2 teaspoons at a time, to keep dough from sticking.) Place dough in a medium bowl; spray top of dough with nonstick cooking spray. Cover, and let rise in a warm draft-free place (85°) until doubled in size, approximately 45 minutes.

FOR FILLING: In a large cast-iron skillet, heat 2 teaspoons olive oil over medium-high heat. Add onion and garlic; cook 2 minutes, stirring frequently. Add pork; cook until browned and crumbly, approximately 7 minutes. Add collard greens, fennel seed, red pepper, tomatoes, and vinegar; cook 1 minute. Remove from heat. Stir in ⅓ cup Cheddar. Set aside.

Preheat oven to 450°. Brush bottom only of a 10-inch (2-inch-deep) cast-iron skillet with remaining 2 teaspoons olive oil; sprinkle with cornmeal.

Lightly punch down dough. Cover, and let stand 5 minutes. On a lightly floured surface, roll dough into a 13-inch circle. Fold dough into quarters; place in prepared skillet. Unfold dough; lightly press into bottom and up sides of skillet. Add pork mixture; sprinkle with remaining 1 cup Cheddar and mozzarella.

Bake until golden brown, approximately 17 minutes. Let stand 5 minutes before serving.

Country Cassoulet with Pork and Boiled Peanuts

YIELD: 6 TO 8 SERVINGS

2   tablespoons canola oil, divided
2   pounds boneless pork shoulder,
    cut into 2-inch cubes
4   ounces country ham or bacon,
    chopped
2   medium carrots, roughly chopped
1   large onion, roughly chopped
1   stalk celery, roughly chopped
2   cloves garlic, minced
4   cups chicken broth
1   cup dry white wine
1   (14.5-ounce) can diced tomatoes
4   sprigs fresh thyme, chopped
2   bay leaves
1   teaspoon ground black pepper
¼   teaspoon crushed red pepper
3   cups shelled boiled peanuts
    (approximately 6 cups unshelled
    peanuts)
2   cups torn day-old French bread
¼   cup chopped fresh parsley
1   tablespoon olive oil

In a large cast-iron Dutch oven, heat 1 tablespoon canola oil over medium-high heat. Add pork shoulder, in batches, and cook until browned on all sides, approximately 4 minutes per side. Remove from pan, and set aside.

Add remaining 1 tablespoon canola oil and country ham or bacon, and cook until browned, approximately 4 minutes. Add carrot, onion, celery, and garlic. Cook until softened, approximately 6 minutes. Add broth, wine, tomatoes, thyme, bay leaves, black pepper, and red pepper. Add pork; bring to a boil, and reduce heat to medium-low. Cover, and simmer until pork is tender, approximately 1 hour. Stir in peanuts.

In the work bowl of a food processor, pulse bread, parsley, and olive oil to form coarse crumbs. Sprinkle on top of stew. Cover, and let simmer on low heat until bread crumbs have thickened sauce, approximately 30 minutes. (Discard bay leaves before serving.)

Country Ham and Gruyère Dutch Baby

YIELD: APPROXIMATELY 6 SERVINGS

½   cup chopped country ham
¼   cup butter
4   large eggs
1   teaspoon ground dry mustard
½   cup all-purpose flour
¼   cup whole milk
¼   cup heavy whipping cream
¼   teaspoon kosher salt
¼   teaspoon ground black pepper
½   cup shredded Gruyère cheese
1   tablespoon chopped fresh chives
½   teaspoon chopped fresh
     tarragon

Preheat oven to 425°.

In a 12-inch cast-iron skillet, cook ham over medium-high heat, stirring frequently, until browned, approximately 10 minutes. Remove from skillet, and set aside. Add butter to skillet; place in oven.

In the work bowl of a food processor, pulse together eggs, mustard, flour, milk, cream, salt, and pepper until combined, 5 to 10 seconds. Remove skillet from oven. Pour egg mixture into skillet.

Bake until puffed and light golden brown, 20 to 25 minutes. Remove from oven. Top with ham, cheese, chives, and tarragon. Serve immediately.

Skillet Pork Chops with Browned Butter, Gravy, and Sage

YIELD: APPROXIMATELY 4 SERVINGS

¼ **cup vegetable oil**

4 **(1-inch-thick) center-cut bone-in pork chops**

½ **cup plus 2 tablespoons all-purpose flour, divided**

1 **teaspoon kosher salt, divided**

½ **teaspoon ground black pepper, divided**

8 **fresh sage leaves**

2 **tablespoons butter**

1½ **teaspoons minced fresh garlic**

1 **to 1½ cups whole milk**

1½ **teaspoons fresh thyme leaves**

In a large cast-iron skillet, heat oil over medium-high heat.

Dredge pork chops in ¼ cup flour, shaking off excess. (You need only a light coating, just enough to keep pork chops dry and to soak up any moisture.)

Evenly sprinkle one side of pork chops with ½ teaspoon salt and ¼ teaspoon pepper. Add pork chops to skillet, seasoned side down. Cook, without moving, 8 to 10 minutes. Evenly season pork chops with remaining ½ teaspoon salt and remaining ¼ teaspoon pepper. Turn pork chops, and cook 8 to 10 minutes. Remove from skillet. Cover loosely with aluminum foil, and set aside.

Add sage leaves to skillet; cook until crisp. Remove from skillet, and set aside. Drain oil, and discard.

Melt butter in skillet. Add garlic, and cook, stirring frequently, 5 minutes. Add remaining ¼ cup plus 2 tablespoons flour to garlic mixture. Whisk in milk, whisking frequently, until thickened and bubbly; stir in thyme. Return pork chops to pan, and garnish with crisp sage leaves. Serve immediately.

Sweet Tea Fried Chicken

YIELD: 4 TO 6 SERVINGS

½ gallon plus 2 cups sweet tea, divided

⅓ cup plus 2 tablespoons kosher salt, divided

1 (3- to 4-pound) whole chicken, cut into pieces

4 cups all-purpose flour

1 teaspoon ground black pepper

½ teaspoon ground red pepper

2 cups whole buttermilk

2 tablespoons hot sauce

5 cups canola oil

In a large nonreactive container, stir together ½ gallon sweet tea and ⅓ cup salt until salt is dissolved. Add chicken pieces to sweet tea mixture. Cover, and refrigerate at least 8 hours or overnight.

Spray the rack of a broiler pan with nonstick cooking spray; place rack in pan. Set aside.

In a shallow dish, combine flour, remaining 2 tablespoons salt, black pepper, and red pepper. In a separate shallow dish, combine buttermilk, remaining 2 cups sweet tea, and hot sauce. Remove chicken from sweet tea mixture; discard tea mixture. Dip each piece in buttermilk mixture; dredge in flour mixture. Place on a wire rack. Dredge chicken in flour mixture again, shaking off excess. Return to wire rack.

Preheat oven to 350°.

In a large deep cast-iron skillet, heat canola oil over medium-high heat until a deep-fry thermometer reads 350°. Working in batches, cook chicken, turning occasionally, until golden brown on all sides, 5 to 8 minutes. (Adjust heat as needed to maintain 350°.) Place chicken on prepared pan.

Bake until a meat thermometer inserted in thickest portion reads 165°, 10 to 20 minutes.

Blackened Redfish

YIELD: 4 TO 6 SERVINGS

2   teaspoons garlic salt
2   teaspoons paprika
½   teaspoon ground black pepper
¼   teaspoon ground red pepper
¼   teaspoon ground white pepper
¼   teaspoon ground dried thyme
¼   teaspoon ground dried basil
¼   teaspoon ground dried oregano
4   (8-ounce) boneless skinless
    redfish fillets
¼   cup melted butter

In a small bowl, stir together garlic salt, paprika, peppers, thyme, basil, and oregano. Evenly coat each fillet with seasoning mix.

Heat a large cast-iron skillet over medium-high heat until hot. Add melted butter. Add 2 fish fillets, and cook until opaque, approximately 6 minutes per side. Baste occasionally with butter from pan. Transfer to a plate, and keep warm. Repeat with remaining fillets.

Slow-Cooked Pork Shoulder with Lemon and Garlic

YIELD: APPROXIMATELY 6 SERVINGS

1   (6-pound) boneless pork shoulder, trimmed
⅓   cup fresh lemon juice
7   tablespoons olive oil, divided
¼   cup minced fresh garlic (about 4 large cloves)
1   teaspoon salt, divided
1   teaspoon ground black pepper, divided
1   large onion, cut into 1-inch pieces
½   cup dry white wine
2   tablespoons chopped fresh oregano
1   lemon, halved
Garnish: fresh oregano

In a large resealable plastic bag, combine pork, lemon juice, 4 tablespoons olive oil, garlic, ½ teaspoon salt, and ½ teaspoon pepper. Seal bag; gently shake to combine. Refrigerate at least 8 hours or up to 12 hours. Remove pork from bag; discard marinade. Tie pork in 2-inch intervals with kitchen twine.

Preheat oven to 325°.

In a large cast-iron Dutch oven, heat 1 tablespoon olive oil over medium-high heat. Add onion; cook until lightly browned, approximately 2 minutes. Remove onion from pan. Add remaining 2 tablespoons olive oil to pan. Add pork; cook until browned on both sides, approximately 3 minutes total. Return onion to pan; add wine, oregano, and remaining ½ teaspoon salt and ½ teaspoon pepper.

Bake, covered, until tender, approximately 2 hours and 30 minutes. Remove pork from pan, and place on a cutting board. Strain pan drippings into a small bowl; discard solids. Squeeze lemon halves over pork. Serve with pan drippings. Garnish with oregano, if desired.

Shrimp and Grits Tart

YIELD: APPROXIMATELY 8 SERVINGS

3   cups water
1   cup yellow quick-cooking grits
2   teaspoons salt, divided
1   (10.5-ounce) package goat cheese, divided
1   tablespoon chopped fresh dill
2   tablespoons butter
4   plum tomatoes, sliced
½   pound medium fresh shrimp, peeled
10 stalks asparagus, ends trimmed and cut into 2-inch pieces
½   teaspoon ground black pepper
Garnish: fresh dill sprigs

Place a 10-inch cast-iron skillet in the oven while it preheats to 400°.

In a medium saucepan, bring 3 cups water, grits, and 1 teaspoon salt to a boil over medium-high heat. Reduce heat, and simmer, stirring frequently, until creamy, approximately 6 minutes. Stir in half of cheese and dill.

Remove skillet from oven; add butter, swirling to coat. Pour grits into hot skillet, and spread in an even layer. Add tomatoes, shrimp, and asparagus. Sprinkle with remaining goat cheese, remaining 1 teaspoon salt, and pepper.

Bake until shrimp are pink and firm, approximately 20 minutes. Garnish with dill. Serve at room temperature.

Quick-and-Easy
Red Beans and Rice

YIELD: 8 TO 10 SERVINGS

3   tablespoons vegetable oil, divided
1   (1-pound) package smoked sausage, cut into 1-inch pieces
½   cup chopped Vidalia onion
½   cup chopped celery
½   cup chopped green bell pepper
2   teaspoons minced fresh garlic
1   (15-ounce) can dark red kidney beans, drained and rinsed
1   (15-ounce) can light red kidney beans, drained and rinsed
1   (15-ounce) can diced tomatoes
2½ teaspoons Creole seasoning
2   teaspoons paprika
3   cups chicken broth
3   cups quick-cooking rice
Garnish: fresh thyme

In a large cast-iron Dutch oven, heat 1 tablespoon oil over medium-high heat. Add sausage, and cook, stirring occasionally, until browned. Remove from pan, and set aside.

Add remaining 2 tablespoons oil, onion, celery, bell pepper, and garlic. Cook, stirring often, until tender, approximately 10 minutes. Add beans, sausage, tomatoes, Creole seasoning, and paprika. Reduce heat to medium-low, and simmer 10 minutes.

In a medium saucepan, bring broth to a boil. Add rice, stirring to combine. Remove from heat. Cover, and let stand 5 minutes. Add rice to bean mixture. Garnish with thyme, if desired.

Grilled Sausage Skewers with Beer-Mustard Sauce

YIELD: 2 TO 4 SERVINGS

⅔ cup stone-ground mustard

⅓ cup beer

3 (6-inch) links sweet or spicy Italian sausage, each cut into 4 pieces

½ medium onion, cut into 1-inch pieces

1 large red or green bell pepper, cut into 1-inch pieces

12 (6-inch) wooden skewers, soaked in water at least 30 minutes

1 tablespoon vegetable oil

½ teaspoon salt

¼ teaspoon ground black pepper

In a small saucepan, combine mustard and beer. Bring to a simmer over medium heat, and cook 2 minutes. Remove from heat.

Thread sausage, onion, and bell pepper onto prepared skewers. Brush skewers with oil; sprinkle with salt and pepper.

Heat a cast-iron griddle over medium heat. Cook until sausage is no longer pink, 15 to 20 minutes, turning skewers occasionally. Serve with mustard sauce.

Savory Cornbread Cobbler

YIELD: APPROXIMATELY 6 SERVINGS

FILLING

4	cups sliced smoked sausage
1	medium Vidalia onion, halved and thinly sliced
1	green bell pepper, cut into thin strips
1	red bell pepper, cut into thin strips
1	tablespoon minced fresh garlic
1	teaspoon dried oregano
¼	teaspoon crushed red pepper
1	(14.5-ounce) can diced tomatoes
1	(16-ounce) can cannellini beans, drained and rinsed
½	cup water
1	teaspoon kosher salt
¼	teaspoon ground black pepper

TOPPING

1	cup stone-ground white or yellow cornmeal
1	cup all-purpose flour
2	teaspoons baking powder
1	teaspoon kosher salt
½	teaspoon baking soda
1½	cups whole buttermilk
¼	cup unsalted butter, melted
1	large egg
1	cup grated Parmesan cheese

Preheat oven to 425°.

FOR FILLING: In a 12-inch cast-iron skillet, cook sausage over medium-high heat until browned, approximately 4 minutes. Remove sausage from skillet. Set aside.

Add onion, bell pepper, garlic, oregano, and crushed red pepper to skillet. Cook, stirring occasionally, until vegetables are tender, approximately 5 minutes. Add tomatoes to skillet; cook 2 minutes. Stir in sausage, beans, ½ cup water, salt, and pepper; bring to a boil. Turn off heat.

FOR TOPPING: In a medium bowl, stir together cornmeal, flour, baking powder, salt, and baking soda. In another medium bowl, stir together buttermilk, melted butter, and egg. Slowly add buttermilk mixture to cornmeal mixture, stirring just until combined. Stir in cheese. Drop batter by heaping tablespoonfuls over sausage mixture.

Bake until topping is golden brown, 15 to 18 minutes.

Skillet Steaks

YIELD: 4 SERVINGS

STEAK

4	beef tenderloin fillets, cut 2 inches thick
1½	teaspoons kosher salt, divided
1	teaspoon ground black pepper, divided
1	cup butter
2	shallots, cut into quarters
6	cloves garlic

HERBED COMPOUND BUTTER

1	cup butter, softened
2	tablespoons finely chopped shallot
2	tablespoons chopped fresh parsley
2	tablespoons chopped fresh chives
2	tablespoons chopped fresh tarragon
1	teaspoon ground black pepper

FOR STEAK: Remove steaks from refrigerator at least 30 minutes before cooking; pat dry with a paper towel. Sprinkle steaks evenly with ¾ teaspoon salt and ½ teaspoon pepper.

Preheat oven to 425°.

Heat a large cast-iron skillet over medium heat. Add butter, and heat until melted. Add shallot and garlic. Cook, stirring occasionally, until tender and browned, approximately 5 minutes. Remove shallot and garlic. Set aside.

Add steaks to skillet, being careful not to overcrowd skillet. Cook 3 to 5 minutes without moving. Sprinkle steaks evenly with remaining ¾ teaspoon salt and remaining ½ teaspoon pepper. Turn steaks over, and return shallot and garlic to pan.

Place skillet in oven. Bake until a meat thermometer inserted in center of steaks reads 125° (or to desired degree of doneness), approximately 5 minutes.

Remove steaks from oven. Let stand 5 minutes. Serve with Herbed Compound Butter.

FOR HERBED COMPOUND BUTTER: In a medium bowl, beat butter at medium-high speed with an electric mixer until creamy. Add shallot, parsley, chives, tarragon, and pepper. Beat until combined. Refrigerate 15 minutes.

Place butter on a large piece of parchment paper. Roll into an 8x2-inch log, twisting parchment at ends. Refrigerate at least 1 hour before using. Store in refrigerator up to 1 week.

Skillet Lasagna

YIELD: APPROXIMATELY 4 SERVINGS

1   (20-ounce) package mild Italian sausage links, casings removed
2   teaspoons minced fresh garlic
1   cup sliced fresh mushrooms
1   (24-ounce) jar tomato basil pasta sauce, divided
¾   cup whole milk ricotta cheese
2   tablespoons chopped fresh oregano, divided
¼   teaspoon salt
¼   teaspoon ground black pepper
1   large egg
7   cooked lasagna noodles
1   cup shredded whole milk mozzarella, divided
½   cup grated Parmesan cheese, divided

Heat a 10-inch (1½- to 2-inch-deep) cast-iron skillet over medium-high heat. Add sausage and garlic, breaking sausage apart with a wooden spoon. Cook, stirring frequently, until sausage is browned and crumbly. Drain, if needed. Place sausage mixture in a large bowl. Set aside.

Add mushrooms to skillet; cook until mushrooms begin to soften, 2 to 3 minutes. Remove from heat. Add mushrooms to sausage mixture. Stir in 2 cups pasta sauce. Reserve remaining pasta sauce (approximately 1 cup). In a small bowl, stir together ricotta, 1 tablespoon oregano, salt, pepper, and egg.

Preheat oven to 350°.

Arrange 3 cooked lasagna noodles in bottom and up sides of skillet. Spread sausage mixture over noodles. Gently spread ricotta mixture over sausage mixture. Sprinkle with ½ cup mozzarella and ¼ cup Parmesan. Arrange remaining 4 lasagna noodles over cheese, trimming ends to fit. Spread remaining pasta sauce over noodles; sprinkle with remaining ½ cup mozzarella and ¼ cup Parmesan.

Bake, covered, 35 minutes. Uncover, and bake 15 minutes more. Let stand at least 10 minutes before serving. Sprinkle with remaining 1 tablespoon oregano.

Skillet-Seared Rainbow Trout with Lemon-Thyme Browned Butter

YIELD: APPROXIMATELY 6 SERVINGS

10 rainbow trout fillets,
   pin bones removed
1½ teaspoons kosher salt, plus
   additional to taste
½ teaspoon ground black pepper,
   plus additional to taste
2 tablespoons all-purpose flour
4 tablespoons unsalted butter
4 cloves garlic, smashed
1 tablespoon capers, drained
10 sprigs fresh thyme
3 tablespoons fresh lemon juice
Garnish: lemon wedges

Spray a large cast-iron skillet with nonstick cooking spray. Heat over medium-high heat.

Season trout with salt and pepper; dust lightly with flour, shaking off excess. Place trout in skillet, skin side down. Cook in batches until golden, approximately 1 minute. Using a spatula, carefully flip trout; cook until golden brown, approximately 2 minutes more. Remove trout from skillet, and place on a serving platter.

Reduce heat to medium-low. Add butter, garlic, capers, and thyme. Cook, stirring occasionally, until butter is browned, approximately 1 minute.

Stir in lemon juice. Season with salt and pepper, if desired. Spoon sauce over trout; serve immediately. Garnish with lemon wedges, if desired.

Lemon-Marinated Fried Chicken

YIELD: APPROXIMATELY 8 SERVINGS

1   (5-pound) whole chicken,
     cut into 8 pieces

BRINE

4   cups water
½   cup salt
¼   cup sugar
6   lemons, halved
6   cloves garlic, smashed
4   bay leaves
1   tablespoon ground black pepper
1   bunch fresh thyme
4   cups ice

CHICKEN

3   cups all-purpose flour
1   teaspoon garlic salt
1   teaspoon onion powder
1   teaspoon ground black pepper
2   cups whole buttermilk
2   large eggs

Peanut oil, for frying
Garnish: fresh thyme

If chicken breasts are large, cut in half.

FOR BRINE: In a large pot, combine 4 cups water, salt, sugar, lemons, garlic, bay leaves, pepper, and thyme. Bring to a boil, and remove from heat. Add ice, and let cool completely.

Add chicken pieces to brine, and refrigerate 8 hours or overnight. Remove chicken from brine; discard brine. Pat chicken dry with paper towels.

FOR CHICKEN: Preheat oven to 350°. Place a wire cooling rack on a rimmed baking sheet, and set aside.

In a large shallow dish, combine flour, garlic salt, onion powder, and pepper. In a large bowl, whisk together buttermilk and eggs.

In a large cast-iron Dutch oven, fill with peanut oil halfway full. Heat over medium-high until a deep-fry thermometer reads 360°.

Dredge chicken pieces in flour mixture, dip in buttermilk, then dredge in flour mixture again. Working in batches, cook chicken until browned and crisp, approximately 6 minutes. (Adjust heat as needed to maintain 360°.) Transfer to prepared rack, and bake until a meat thermometer inserted in center of breasts reads 165°, 10 to 15 minutes. Garnish with thyme, if desired.

Goat Cheese, Mushroom, and Spinach Frittata

YIELD: 4 TO 6 SERVINGS

4	large eggs
¾	cup grated Asiago cheese
1	tablespoon chopped fresh rosemary
¼	teaspoon kosher salt
¼	teaspoon ground black pepper
⅛	teaspoon ground red pepper
3	tablespoons olive oil
1	Vidalia onion, chopped
1	(8-ounce) package sliced mushrooms
1	(6-ounce) bag fresh baby spinach
1	(4-ounce) package goat cheese, crumbled

Garnish: fresh rosemary

Preheat oven to 375°.

In a large bowl, whisk together eggs, Asiago, rosemary, salt, and peppers. Set aside.

In a 10-inch cast-iron skillet, heat olive oil over medium-high heat. Add onion; cook, stirring frequently, until tender, approximately 5 minutes. Add mushrooms, and cook, stirring frequently, until tender, approximately 3 minutes.

Add spinach, and cook, stirring occasionally, until wilted, approximately 5 minutes. Add egg mixture to onion mixture, whisking to combine. Sprinkle with goat cheese.

Bake until golden brown and set, approximately 30 minutes. Let cool in pan 5 minutes. Garnish with rosemary, if desired.

Southern-Fried Fish and Chips

YIELD: APPROXIMATELY 4 SERVINGS

CHIPS

1   large sweet potato, very thinly
     sliced
Vegetable oil, for frying
1   teaspoon kosher salt

FISH

½   cup whole milk
1   large egg
3½   cups all-purpose flour, divided
2   teaspoons kosher salt, divided
2   teaspoons Creole seasoning
1   teaspoon baking powder
1¾   cups sparkling water
1½   pounds red snapper fillets,
     skinned and cut into about
     3x1-inch strips
Malt vinegar, to serve

FOR CHIPS: In a large bowl filled with ice water, place sliced sweet potato; let stand 15 minutes. Drain, and thoroughly pat dry. Line a plate with paper towels. Set aside.

In a large cast-iron Dutch oven, pour oil to halfway full. Heat over medium heat until a deep-fry thermometer reads 350°. Cook potatoes in batches, turning occasionally, until crisp and golden brown, approximately 2 minutes. Remove chips with a slotted spoon, and let drain on paper towels. Sprinkle with salt. (Turn off heat if not immediately frying fish.)

FOR FISH: In a shallow dish, whisk together milk and egg. In another dish, combine 2 cups flour and 1 teaspoon salt. In a medium bowl, whisk together remaining 1½ cups flour, remaining 1 teaspoon salt, Creole seasoning, and baking powder. Whisk in 1¾ cups sparkling water.

Heat oil over medium-high heat until a deep-fry thermometer reads 350°. Working with approximately 4 fish strips at a time, dip in milk mixture. Dredge in flour mixture. Dip fish in batter; gently place in hot oil. Cook, turning occasionally, until golden brown, approximately 3 minutes. (Adjust heat as needed to maintain 350°.) Remove fish with a slotted spoon, and let drain on paper towels. Serve fish with chips and malt vinegar.

Chicken with Roasted Vegetables

YIELD: 6 TO 8 SERVINGS

LEMON VINAIGRETTE

$\frac{3}{4}$ **cup extra-virgin olive oil**

$\frac{1}{4}$ **cup white wine vinegar**

1   **tablespoon lemon zest**

2   **tablespoons fresh lemon juice**

1   **tablespoon chopped fresh tarragon**

1   **tablespoon chopped fresh dill**

$\frac{1}{4}$ **teaspoon kosher salt**

$\frac{1}{8}$ **teaspoon ground black pepper**

CHICKEN

$1\frac{1}{2}$ **pounds fingerling potatoes, cut in half lengthwise**

1   **(7-ounce) package baby rainbow carrots, cut in half lengthwise**

1   **fennel bulb, cut into eighths**

6   **cloves garlic**

3   **bay leaves**

Lemon Vinaigrette (recipe precedes)

3   **teaspoons kosher salt, divided**

$1\frac{3}{4}$ **teaspoons ground black pepper, divided**

$\frac{1}{4}$ **cup lemon-infused olive oil**

1   **(4-pound) whole chicken, split in half**

FOR LEMON VINAIGRETTE: In a small bowl, whisk together olive oil, vinegar, and lemon zest and juice. Add tarragon, dill, salt, and pepper, whisking to combine. Set aside.

FOR CHICKEN: Preheat oven to 400°.

In a large bowl, combine potato, carrot, fennel, garlic, and bay leaves. Pour Lemon Vinaigrette over vegetables, and add 1 teaspoon salt and $\frac{3}{4}$ teaspoon pepper, stirring to combine.

Place vegetables in a large 3-inch-deep cast-iron skillet. Rub chicken with olive oil. Sprinkle both sides evenly with remaining 2 teaspoons salt and 1 teaspoon pepper. Place chicken on top of vegetables.

Bake until a meat thermometer inserted in thickest part of thigh reads 165°, 1 to $1\frac{1}{2}$ hours.

Remove from oven. Transfer chicken to a serving platter. Stir vegetables to coat with pan juices. (Discard bay leaves before serving.) Serve immediately.

Soups

SANDWICHES & SUCH

Turkey and Seafood Gumbo

YIELD: APPROXIMATELY 12 SERVINGS

1½ cups all-purpose flour
1¼ cups vegetable oil
3   cups chopped yellow onion
1½ cups chopped red bell pepper
1½ cups chopped celery
2   pounds andouille sausage
     (Cajun smoked sausage),
     cut into ¼-inch-thick slices
4   bay leaves
3   quarts turkey or chicken broth
1   pound fresh crab claws
1   pound shucked oysters
1½ pounds large fresh shrimp, peeled
     and deveined (tails left on)
2   cups chopped cooked turkey
Hot cooked rice

In a large enamel-coated cast-iron Dutch oven, combine flour and oil over medium heat. Cook, whisking constantly, until flour mixture turns dark brown, approximately 15 minutes. Add onion, bell pepper, celery, sausage, and bay leaves, stirring until well combined. Gradually add broth, and stir until well combined. Bring to a boil. Reduce heat to medium-low, and simmer, uncovered, 1½ hours, stirring occasionally.

Add crab claws and oysters; cook 10 minutes. Add shrimp and turkey; cook until shrimp are pink and firm, approximately 5 minutes. Remove bay leaves, and discard.

Serve with hot cooked rice.

Patty Melts with Secret Sauce

YIELD: 6 SERVINGS

SECRET SAUCE

¼ cup Dijon mustard

¼ cup mayonnaise

1 tablespoon barbecue sauce

½ teaspoon hot sauce

CARAMELIZED ONIONS

2 tablespoons unsalted butter

3 medium Vidalia onions, thinly sliced

SANDWICH

1½ pounds ground beef

2 teaspoons Worcestershire sauce

1 teaspoon kosher salt

½ teaspoon ground black pepper

12 slices sourdough bread

½ cup Secret Sauce (recipe precedes)

1 cup Caramelized Onions (recipe precedes)

6 slices Cheddar cheese

6 tablespoons unsalted butter

FOR SECRET SAUCE: In a small bowl, stir together mustard, mayonnaise, barbecue sauce, and hot sauce.

FOR CARAMELIZED ONIONS: In a medium cast-iron skillet, melt butter over medium heat. Add onion. Cook, stirring occasionally, until onion is soft and golden brown, approximately 35 minutes.

FOR SANDWICH: In a large bowl, combine ground beef, Worcestershire, salt, and pepper. Shape ground beef into 6 oval patties.

In a large cast-iron skillet, cook patties over medium-high heat until browned and cooked through, approximately 2 minutes per side. Remove skillet from heat. Remove patties from skillet; wipe out skillet.

Layer 1 bread slice with 1 tablespoon Secret Sauce, 2 to 3 tablespoons Caramelized Onions, 1 slice cheese, 1 patty, and another 1 tablespoon Secret Sauce. Top with another bread slice. Repeat with remaining bread, Secret Sauce, Caramelized Onions, cheese, and patties.

Heat skillet over medium-high heat. Melt 2 tablespoons butter in skillet. Working in batches, cook sandwiches, flipping once, until golden brown and heated through, approximately 3 minutes per side. Add remaining butter to skillet as needed.

Roasted Cauliflower Soup

YIELD: 6 TO 8 SERVINGS

1   large head cauliflower, trimmed
    and diced
3   tablespoons vegetable oil

SOUP

6   slices bacon, cut into 1-inch pieces
1   cup chopped Vidalia onion
Roasted Cauliflower (recipe precedes)
2   cups chicken broth
1   tablespoon chopped fresh thyme
1   teaspoon salt
½   teaspoon ground black pepper
¼   teaspoon ground nutmeg
⅛   teaspoon ground white pepper
2½ cups whole milk
½   cup heavy whipping cream
1   cup grated Parmesan cheese
Garnish: fresh thyme, Parmesan
    cheese

Preheat oven to 400°.

FOR ROASTED CAULIFLOWER: Line a rimmed baking sheet with aluminum foil. Set aside. In a large bowl, combine cauliflower and oil, stirring to combine.

Place cauliflower on prepared pan. Bake until cauliflower is browned, 25 to 30 minutes. Remove from oven, and let cool.

FOR SOUP: In a large cast-iron Dutch oven, cook bacon over medium-high heat until crisp. Remove with a slotted spoon, and let cool. Crumble, and set aside. Reserve rendered bacon fat in pan.

Add onion to pan. Cook, stirring often, until tender, approximately 5 minutes. Add Roasted Cauliflower, broth, thyme, salt, black pepper, nutmeg, and white pepper. Cook, stirring occasionally, 15 minutes. Remove from heat, and let cool to room temperature.

In the container of a blender, purée soup in batches, if necessary, until smooth. Return to pan. Add milk, cream, and cheese. Cook over medium heat until soup is heated through and cheese is melted.

Garnish with bacon, thyme, and cheese, if desired.

Vegetable-Beef Stew

YIELD: APPROXIMATELY 8 SERVINGS

3 pounds beef stew meat
⅓ cup all-purpose flour
¼ cup olive oil
1 large onion, chopped
2 cloves garlic, minced
3¾ cups beef broth
1½ cups dry red wine
1 tablespoon dried basil
1 tablespoon dried parsley
2 teaspoons salt
1 teaspoon ground black pepper
1 cup frozen green peas, thawed
2 large baking or russet potatoes, peeled and cut into 1-inch pieces
3 large carrots, peeled and chopped
3 stalks celery, chopped
1 (8-ounce) package sliced fresh mushrooms

Place beef and flour in a resealable plastic bag. Seal bag, and shake vigorously to coat beef.

In a large cast-iron Dutch oven, heat olive oil over medium-high heat. Add beef, and cook until browned, stirring occasionally.

Add onion and garlic. Cook until onion is tender, approximately 5 minutes.

Stir in broth, wine, basil, parsley, salt, and pepper. Cover, reduce heat to low, and simmer 2 hours, stirring occasionally.

Add peas, potato, carrot, celery, and mushrooms. Cover, and simmer until vegetables are tender, approximately 30 minutes.

Onion, Bean, and Bacon Soup

YIELD: APPROXIMATELY 12 SERVINGS

6   slices bacon, cut into ½-inch pieces
5   cups thinly sliced yellow onion
¼   cup all-purpose flour
6   cups beef broth
1   cup red wine
3   tablespoons adobo sauce (from 1 can chipotle peppers in adobo)
2   teaspoons kosher salt
1   (15-ounce) can cannellini beans, drained and rinsed
1   tablespoon olive oil
12 (½-inch-thick) baguette slices
12 slices provolone cheese

In a large cast-iron Dutch oven, cook bacon over medium-high heat until cooked through but not crisp. Remove with a slotted spoon, and set aside. Reserve 3 tablespoons rendered bacon fat in pan.

Add onion to pan, and cook over medium-high heat, stirring frequently, until just beginning to brown, 15 to 20 minutes.

Sift flour over onion. Cook until thickened, 2 to 3 minutes. Add broth, wine, adobo sauce, and salt, stirring well. Bring to a boil over medium-high heat. Reduce heat to medium-low, and simmer 15 minutes, stirring often. Add beans to onion mixture, stirring well. Return to a simmer; cook 5 minutes. Remove from heat. Let cool 10 minutes.

Preheat oven to 400°. Brush olive oil on both sides of baguette slices, and place on a baking sheet. Bake until golden brown, approximately 6 minutes.

Increase oven temperature to broil.

Spoon 1 cup soup into an oven-safe serving bowl. Top with 1 baguette slice. Place 1 slice provolone on top of bread. Top with desired amount of reserved bacon. Repeat with remaining soup, baguette, cheese, and bacon. Broil, 5 inches from heat, until cheese is browned, 2 to 3 minutes.

Corn Cakes with Roasted Tomato-Pecan Chutney

YIELD: APPROXIMATELY 20 CORN CAKES

ROASTED TOMATO-PECAN CHUTNEY

- 8   medium plum tomatoes, halved lengthwise (about 1½ pounds)
- 1   tablespoon vegetable oil
- ½   teaspoon salt, divided
- ½   teaspoon ground black pepper, divided
- ½   cup toasted pecans, chopped
- 2   teaspoons firmly packed light brown sugar
- 1½   teaspoons red wine vinegar
- ¼   teaspoon smoked paprika

CORN CAKES

- 1   cup stone-ground white or yellow cornmeal
- 2   tablespoons all-purpose flour
- 2   tablespoons chopped green onion
- ½   teaspoon baking powder
- ½   teaspoon salt
- ¼   teaspoon ground black pepper
- ⅔   cup whole buttermilk
- 4   tablespoons vegetable oil, divided
- 1   large egg

FOR ROASTED TOMATO-PECAN CHUTNEY: Preheat oven to 300°. In a large cast-iron skillet, place tomatoes, cut sides up. Drizzle with oil, and sprinkle with ¼ teaspoon each salt and pepper.

Bake until tomatoes are very tender but still hold their shape, approximately 3 hours. Remove from oven; let cool slightly. Turn tomatoes over; gently remove peels.

In the work bowl of a food processor, place tomatoes; pulse until almost smooth, approximately 3 times. Spoon tomato mixture into a bowl. Stir in remaining ¼ teaspoon each salt and pepper, pecans, brown sugar, vinegar, and paprika.

FOR CORN CAKES: In a medium bowl, combine cornmeal, flour, green onion, baking powder, salt, and pepper. Add buttermilk, 2 tablespoons oil, and egg; stir well.

On the smooth side of a cast-iron griddle, heat 1 tablespoon oil over medium heat. For each corn cake, spoon 1 tablespoon batter, 1 inch apart, onto griddle. Cook until bubbles appear on surface and bottoms are lightly browned, 1½ to 2 minutes. Turn corn cakes; cook until done, approximately 1 minute. Add remaining 1 tablespoon oil to griddle, if needed, to cook remaining corn cakes. Serve with Roasted Tomato-Pecan Chutney.

Braised Beef Chili

YIELD: 8 TO 10 SERVINGS

2   tablespoons canola oil

1   (2½- to 3-pound) boneless chuck
     roast

3   teaspoons salt, divided

¾   teaspoon ground black pepper,
     divided

2   poblano peppers

1   red or green bell pepper

3   cups chopped Vidalia onion
     (about 2 medium onions)

1   tablespoon minced chiles in adobo

2   tablespoons tomato paste

1   tablespoon dried oregano

1   teaspoon ground cumin

¼   teaspoon garlic powder

⅛   teaspoon ground coriander

1   cup dry white wine

3   cups water

2   (14.5-ounce) cans diced tomatoes

2   tablespoons apple cider vinegar

1   (15.5-ounce) can red kidney beans,
     drained and rinsed

Garnish: shredded Cheddar cheese,
     sour cream

Preheat oven to 350°.

In a large cast-iron Dutch oven, heat canola oil over high heat. Season beef with 2 teaspoons salt and ½ teaspoon pepper. Add beef to pan; cook until browned on all sides, approximately 3 minutes per side. Remove from pan. Set aside.

Add whole poblano and bell peppers to pan. Cook, turning occasionally, until charred on all sides, approximately 8 minutes. Remove from pan. Set aside.

Reduce heat to medium. Add onion, stirring to scrape browned and blackened bits from bottom of pan. Cook, stirring occasionally, until softened, approximately 6 minutes. Meanwhile, using a knife, carefully scrape peppers to remove charred skin, and discard. Halve peppers lengthwise; remove and discard stems and seeds. Coarsely chop peppers.

Add peppers, chiles in adobo, tomato paste, oregano, cumin, garlic powder, and coriander to pan. Cook approximately 2 minutes, stirring constantly. Add wine, scraping to remove browned bits from bottom of pan. Cook 2 minutes, stirring occasionally. Add 3 cups water, tomato, vinegar, remaining 1 teaspoon salt, remaining ¼ teaspoon pepper, and beef. Bring to a boil. Cover, and place in oven.

Bake until beef is tender, approximately 2 hours and 30 minutes. Carefully place beef on a cutting board. Using two forks, shred beef, and return to pan. Stir in kidney beans. Garnish with cheese and sour cream, if desired.

Buttermilk Cornbread

YIELD: APPROXIMATELY 6 SERVINGS

2¼ cups plain white or yellow
    cornmeal
1½ teaspoons baking powder
½   teaspoon baking soda
¾   teaspoon salt
1⅔ cups whole buttermilk
4   tablespoons vegetable oil,
    divided
1   large egg

Preheat oven to 450°.

In a large bowl, combine cornmeal, baking powder, baking soda, and salt. In a small bowl, whisk together buttermilk, 2 tablespoons oil, and egg. Make a well in center of dry ingredients; add buttermilk mixture, stirring just until moistened.

In a 10-inch cast-iron skillet, heat remaining 2 tablespoons oil over medium-high heat. Remove from heat, and carefully pour batter into hot oil in skillet. (Do not stir.)

Bake until cornbread is golden brown and a wooden pick inserted in center comes out clean, 17 to 20 minutes. Serve warm.

Hearty Vegetable Soup with Drop Dumplings

YIELD: APPROXIMATELY 8 SERVINGS

SOUP

2	slices salt pork or bacon
1	cup chopped onion
¾	cup thinly sliced carrot
½	cup chopped yellow bell pepper
2	teaspoons minced fresh garlic
4	cups water
2	cups chicken broth
1	cup chopped red potato
¾	teaspoon salt
¼	teaspoon ground black pepper
2	cups chopped fresh kale
1	(14.5-ounce) can diced tomatoes with rosemary and oregano, drained
1	tablespoon chopped fresh thyme
¼	teaspoon smoked paprika
2	teaspoons apple cider vinegar

DUMPLINGS

2	cups plus 2 tablespoons all-purpose flour, divided
4	teaspoons baking powder
1	teaspoon salt
¼	teaspoon ground black pepper, plus additional to taste
⅔	cup whole milk
3	tablespoons vegetable oil
1	large egg

Garnish: fresh thyme

FOR SOUP: In a 5-quart or larger cast-iron Dutch oven, cook salt pork over medium heat until browned. Discard pork; reserve rendered fat in pan. Add onion, carrot, bell pepper, and garlic. Cook until vegetables begin to soften, approximately 5 minutes. Add 4 cups water, broth, potato, salt, and pepper; bring to a boil. Cover, and reduce heat to medium-low. Cook until potato is tender, approximately 8 minutes. Add kale, tomatoes, thyme, paprika, and vinegar; cook 5 minutes.

FOR DUMPLINGS: In a large bowl, whisk together 2 cups flour, baking powder, salt, and pepper. In a small bowl, whisk together milk, oil, and egg. Add milk mixture to flour mixture. Stir until a soft dough forms and pulls away from sides of bowl (add remaining 2 tablespoons flour, if necessary). With floured hands, roll dough into approximately 25 (1-inch) balls.

Bring soup to a boil over medium-high heat; quickly drop dough balls into soup. Cover, and reduce heat to medium-low. Simmer until dumplings are puffed and cooked through, approximately 15 minutes. Sprinkle with additional pepper and thyme, if desired. Serve immediately.

Crawfish and Corn Chowder

YIELD: APPROXIMATELY 10 SERVINGS

4   tablespoons corn oil
4   tablespoons butter
2   cups diced Vidalia onion
1   cup diced celery
½   cup chopped poblano pepper
1   tablespoon minced fresh garlic
½   cup all-purpose flour
½   cup dry white wine
1   quart seafood stock
1   (16-ounce) package frozen corn,
       thawed
1½ pounds red potato, chopped
1   (14.5-ounce) can crushed
       tomatoes
1   (8-ounce) can tomato sauce
1   (16-ounce) package frozen
       crawfish tails, thawed
2   bay leaves
1   tablespoon chopped fresh thyme
2   teaspoons kosher salt
2   teaspoons Cajun seasoning
2   teaspoons ground black pepper
1½ cups heavy whipping cream
1   tablespoon chopped fresh parsley

In a large cast-iron Dutch oven, heat corn oil over medium-high heat. Add butter, and let melt. Add onion, celery, poblano, and garlic; cook until tender, approximately 10 minutes. Add flour, and cook, stirring constantly, 5 minutes. Add wine and stock, whisking to combine. Bring mixture to a boil, reduce heat to medium, and simmer 15 minutes.

Add corn, potato, tomato, tomato sauce, crawfish, bay leaves, thyme, salt, Cajun seasoning, and pepper. Cook, stirring frequently, 30 minutes. Add cream, stirring to combine. Cook 10 minutes more. Remove from heat, and add parsley. Remove bay leaves, and discard.

Panini with Prosciutto and Sage Pesto

YIELD: 4 SERVINGS

1   cup fresh sage leaves
⅔   cup walnut halves, toasted
½   cup grated Parmesan cheese
½   teaspoon lemon zest
½   teaspoon salt
⅛   teaspoon ground black pepper
1   small clove garlic
½   to ⅔ cup extra-virgin olive oil
8   slices sourdough bread
8   thin slices prosciutto
8   thin slices tomato, patted dry
16   thin slices whole milk
     mozzarella cheese
2   tablespoons vegetable oil

In the work bowl of a food processor, combine sage, walnuts, Parmesan, lemon zest, salt, pepper, and garlic. Pulse until minced, 6 to 8 times. With food processor running, slowly add ½ cup olive oil until mixture is smooth. Add remaining 2 tablespoons olive oil, if needed. Scrape into a small bowl or jar. Spread 1 tablespoon sage pesto over 1 side of each bread slice.

Divide prosciutto, tomato, and mozzarella among 4 bread slices. Cover with remaining 4 bread slices, pesto side down.

Brush the flat side of a cast-iron griddle with vegetable oil; heat over medium heat. Place sandwiches on griddle; brush tops with olive oil. Press sandwiches with a spatula or another cast-iron pan to flatten. Cook, pressing occasionally, until bread is golden brown and cheese melts, approximately 3 minutes. Turn sandwiches over; flatten with spatula. Cook until golden brown.

Leek and Potato Soup with Bacon

YIELD: APPROXIMATELY 8 SERVINGS

6   slices bacon, cut into
    ¼-inch pieces
3   leeks, halved lengthwise, rinsed,
    and sliced (about 6 cups)
2   cloves garlic, minced
4   cups diced red potato (about
    1½ pounds)
1   tablespoon fresh thyme leaves
8   cups chicken broth
½   teaspoon kosher salt
¼   teaspoon ground black pepper
½   cup heavy whipping cream

In a large cast-iron Dutch oven, cook bacon over medium heat until crisp. Remove with a slotted spoon, and let cool. Set aside. Drain all but 2 tablespoons rendered bacon fat from pan.

Add leek and garlic to pan. Cook, stirring occasionally, until tender, 5 to 6 minutes. Add potato, thyme, broth, salt, and pepper. Bring to a boil, and reduce heat to low. Simmer until potato is tender, approximately 20 minutes.

Using a potato masher, roughly mash potato. Stir in cream. Top with bacon.

Cheddar-Chile Hush Puppies

YIELD: APPROXIMATELY 16 HUSH PUPPIES

HUSH PUPPIES

Canola oil, for frying

½ cup stone-ground white
    or yellow cornmeal

½ cup all-purpose flour

1 teaspoon baking powder

½ teaspoon kosher salt

¼ teaspoon baking soda

¾ cup whole buttermilk

2 tablespoons unsalted butter,
    melted

1 large egg

1 cup shredded sharp Cheddar
    cheese

2 tablespoons diced mild green
    chiles

DIPPING SAUCE

¼ cup mayonnaise

2 tablespoons whole buttermilk

1 tablespoon sour cream

1 tablespoon diced mild green chiles

1 teaspoon hot sauce

FOR HUSH PUPPIES: In a large cast-iron Dutch oven, pour canola oil to halfway full. Heat over medium-high heat until a deep-fry thermometer reads 350°. Line a plate with paper towels. Set aside.

In a medium bowl, stir together cornmeal, flour, baking powder, salt, and baking soda. In a separate medium bowl, stir together buttermilk, melted butter, and egg. Slowly add buttermilk mixture to cornmeal mixture, stirring just until combined. Stir in cheese and chiles.

Drop batter by tablespoonfuls into hot oil. Fry, in batches, until golden brown, approximately 2 minutes per side. (Adjust heat as needed to maintain 350°.) Let drain on paper towels.

FOR DIPPING SAUCE: In a small bowl, stir together mayonnaise, buttermilk, sour cream, chiles, and hot sauce. Serve with hush puppies.

Winter Vegetable Soup

YIELD: APPROXIMATELY 6 SERVINGS

3 tablespoons vegetable oil
3 tablespoons butter
1 cup sliced Vidalia onion
1 cup sliced carrot
½ cup chopped celery
1 clove garlic, minced
1 (16-ounce) bag dried white
   kidney beans, sorted, rinsed
   soaked (see note)
3 cups reserved water from
   soaking beans
1 quart vegetable broth
1 cup chopped parsnip
1 cup chopped butternut squash
1 cup chopped turnip
1 cup chopped sweet potato
2 tablespoons chopped fresh
   rosemary
2 teaspoons kosher salt
1 teaspoon ground black pepper
1 (5-ounce) bag fresh spinach

In a large enamel-coated cast-iron Dutch oven, heat oil over medium-high heat. Add butter, and let melt. Add onion, carrot, celery, and garlic; cook until tender, approximately 10 minutes.

Add soaked beans and 3 cups reserved water from soaking beans. (Add water to make 3 cups, if necessary.) Cook 45 minutes, adding water, if necessary. Add broth, parsnip, butternut squash, turnip, sweet potato, rosemary, salt, and pepper. Simmer over medium-high heat until vegetables are tender, 15 to 20 minutes. Stir in spinach, and cook until wilted.

Note: To soak beans, place in a large saucepan, and cover with 6 to 8 cups water. Let stand 8 hours or overnight. Drain, and rinse beans, reserving water from soaking.

Sides

Black-Eyed Peas with Tomatoes

YIELD: 6 TO 8 SERVINGS

3   **slices bacon, chopped**

5   **cups fresh black-eyed peas**

4   **cups water**

2   **cups quartered cherry tomatoes**

½   **cup plus 2 tablespoons chopped green onion, divided**

2   **bay leaves**

1   **teaspoon salt**

1   **teaspoon ground black pepper**

In a medium cast-iron Dutch oven, cook bacon over medium-high heat until crisp. Remove with a slotted spoon, and let cool. Set aside. Reserve rendered bacon fat in pan.

Add peas and 4 cups water to pan. Bring to a boil over medium-high heat. Reduce heat to medium-low. Add tomatoes, ½ cup green onion, and bay leaves.

Simmer until peas are tender, approximately 1 hour, adding additional water, if necessary. Season with salt and pepper. Remove bay leaves, and discard. Sprinkle with bacon and remaining 2 tablespoons green onion.

Creamed Corn

YIELD: 4 TO 6 SERVINGS

5	**large ears fresh corn**
2	**cups whole milk**
3	**tablespoons butter**
1	**cup chopped onion**
2	**teaspoons cornstarch**
2	**teaspoons chopped fresh thyme**
¾	**teaspoon salt**
½	**teaspoon ground black pepper**

Cut kernels from corn into a medium bowl (about 4½ cups kernels). Using the dull side of knife, scrape milk and pulp from cobs into bowl. In the container of a blender, purée 1 cup corn kernels and milk. Set aside.

In a 10-inch cast-iron skillet, melt butter over medium heat. Add onion and remaining 3½ cups corn to pan; cook until onion begins to soften, approximately 7 minutes. Add puréed corn mixture to skillet; bring to a simmer. Reduce heat to medium-low, and cook, stirring occasionally, until tender, approximately 15 minutes.

Add cornstarch, thyme, salt, and pepper to corn mixture; stir well. Cook, stirring frequently, until thickened, approximately 5 minutes.

Fried Okra

YIELD: 8 TO 10 SERVINGS

Vegetable oil, for frying

2   cups plain yellow cornmeal

½   cup all-purpose flour

2   tablespoons Creole seasoning

2   teaspoons seasoned salt

½   teaspoon ground red pepper

1   large egg, lightly beaten

¾   cup whole buttermilk

1   pound fresh okra, stems removed and cut into ½-inch slices

In a large cast-iron skillet or Dutch oven, pour oil to a depth of 2 inches; heat oil over medium-high heat until a deep-fry thermometer reads 375°.

In a shallow dish, combine cornmeal, flour, Creole seasoning, seasoned salt, and red pepper, mixing well.

In a separate shallow dish, whisk together egg and buttermilk.

Working in batches, dip okra in buttermilk mixture, allowing excess to drip off. Dredge in cornmeal mixture, tossing gently to coat. Shake gently to remove excess. Fry okra 3 to 4 minutes, being careful not to overcrowd pan. (Adjust heat as needed to maintain 375°.) Let drain on paper towels.

Roasted Cauliflower
with Coriander and Lime

YIELD: APPROXIMATELY 4 SERVINGS

6   cups cauliflower florets
3   tablespoons extra-virgin olive oil
1   tablespoon minced shallot
1   teaspoon ground coriander
1   teaspoon salt
¼   teaspoon ground black pepper
1   clove garlic, minced
¼   cup chopped roasted salted peanuts
2   tablespoons chopped fresh cilantro
4   lime wedges

Preheat oven to 450°.

In a large bowl, combine cauliflower, olive oil, shallot, coriander, salt, pepper, and garlic. Divide mixture evenly among 4 shallow (2-cup) cast-iron baking dishes.

Bake until cauliflower is tender and lightly browned, approximately 20 minutes, stirring once. Sprinkle with peanuts and cilantro. Squeeze 1 lime wedge over each dish before serving.

Pinto Beans with Smoked Ham Hock

YIELD: APPROXIMATELY 6 SERVINGS

1   pound dried pinto beans,
       sorted and rinsed

6   cups water, divided

3½ teaspoons salt, divided

2   cups chicken broth

1   cup chopped onion

¼   teaspoon crushed red pepper

1   smoked ham hock

1   clove garlic, minced

In an enamel-coated cast-iron Dutch oven (see note), combine beans, 4 cups water, and 2 teaspoons salt. Bring to a boil; cover, and remove from heat. Let stand 1 hour.

Drain beans, and return to pot. Add remaining 2 cups water, remaining 1½ teaspoons salt, broth, onion, red pepper, ham hock, and garlic. Bring to a boil; reduce heat to medium-low. Simmer, partially covered, until beans are very tender, 2 hours to 2 hours and 30 minutes, stirring occasionally. Add additional water, if necessary.

Note: We recommend cooking pinto beans in an enamel-coated cast-iron pan. Cooking in exposed cast iron will give the beans a grayish color.

Layered Field Pea Salad

YIELD: APPROXIMATELY 6 SERVINGS

1   pound fresh okra, halved
     lengthwise
1   teaspoon kosher salt
1   teaspoon ground black pepper
½   pound fresh lady peas, cooked
½   pound fresh pink-eyed peas,
     cooked
½   pound fresh baby lima beans,
     cooked
½   cup sherry vinegar
¼   cup extra-virgin olive oil
1   (12-ounce) container heirloom
     cherry tomatoes, halved or
     quartered
Garnish: fresh dill, oregano,
     marjoram

Spray a cast-iron grill pan with nonstick nonflammable cooking spray. Heat pan over medium-high heat. Cook okra, turning occasionally, until tender and slightly browned, approximately 6 minutes. Add salt and pepper. Remove from pan, and set aside.

In a large bowl, combine peas, beans, vinegar, and olive oil, stirring to coat.

Arrange pea mixture on a large platter. Top with okra and tomatoes. Garnish with dill, oregano, and marjoram, if desired.

Pimiento Cheese-Stuffed Jalapeños

YIELD: 1 DOZEN JALAPEÑOS

2 ounces cream cheese, softened
1 tablespoon mayonnaise
1 (4-ounce) jar diced pimientos, drained
1 cup shredded sharp Cheddar cheese
¾ teaspoon salt, divided
¼ teaspoon ground black pepper
⅛ teaspoon garlic powder
2 teaspoons canola oil
6 medium jalapeño peppers, halved lengthwise (see note)
4 slices bacon, cooked and crumbled
2 tablespoons chopped green onion

Preheat oven to 375°.

In a medium bowl, combine cream cheese, mayonnaise, and pimientos; stir well. Stir in Cheddar, ½ teaspoon salt, pepper, and garlic powder. Set aside.

In a 10-inch cast-iron skillet, heat canola oil over medium heat. Add peppers, cut side down. Cook until edges are lightly browned, approximately 2 minutes. Remove from heat. Turn peppers over; sprinkle with remaining ¼ teaspoon salt. Spoon approximately 1 tablespoon pimiento mixture into each pepper half.

Bake until peppers are tender and cheese melts, approximately 15 minutes. Sprinkle with bacon and green onion.

Note: For less heat, remove seeds from jalapeños before cooking.

Potato Soufflés

YIELD: 6 SERVINGS

2½ pounds baking or russet potatoes, peeled and cut into 1-inch pieces (about 3 large potatoes)
1   tablespoon salt
½   cup unsalted butter, softened
4   ounces cream cheese, softened
1   cup sour cream
2   teaspoons garlic salt
2   large eggs
Paprika

Preheat oven to 350°.

In a large saucepan, add potatoes, salt, and water to cover. Bring to a boil over high heat. Reduce heat to medium, and simmer until fork-tender, approximately 20 minutes. Drain, and place in a large bowl.

Add butter, cream cheese, sour cream, and garlic salt. Beat at low speed with an electric mixer until combined. Let cool 10 minutes.

Add eggs. Increase mixer speed to medium, and beat until fluffy, approximately 30 seconds. Spoon potato mixture into 6 oval cast-iron mini servers, and sprinkle with paprika.

Bake until lightly browned, approximately 20 minutes.

Grits-Fried Dill Pickles

YIELD: APPROXIMATELY 4 SERVINGS

Vegetable oil, for frying
1   cup whole milk
2   tablespoons spicy brown
      mustard
2   teaspoons hot sauce, plus more
      for serving
1   cup all-purpose flour
½   cup stone-ground grits
1   teaspoon salt, plus more for
      seasoning
1   (16-ounce) jar dill pickle slices,
      drained
Ground black pepper
Hot sauce (optional)

In a small cast-iron Dutch oven, pour oil to halfway full. Heat oil over medium-high heat until a deep-fry thermometer reads 350°.

In a medium bowl, whisk together milk, mustard, and hot sauce. In a shallow dish, combine flour, grits, and salt. Working in batches, dip pickle slices into milk mixture, then into grits mixture, tossing gently to coat.

Fry in batches until golden brown, 2 to 3 minutes, turning occasionally. (Adjust heat as needed to maintain 350°.) Remove pickles from hot oil with a slotted spoon; let drain on paper towels. Season with salt and pepper. Serve with hot sauce, if desired.

Beer-Battered Onion Rings
with Mustard Sauce

YIELD: APPROXIMATELY 4 SERVINGS

ONION RINGS

1   **large white onion, cut into ½-inch-thick slices**

1   **cup plus 2 tablespoons self-rising flour, divided**

⅓   **cup plain white or yellow cornmeal**

1   **teaspoon salt, divided**

1   **cup beer**

1   **teaspoon hot sauce**

Vegetable oil, for frying

SAUCE

⅔   **cup spicy brown mustard**

¼   **cup red wine vinegar**

2   **tablespoons honey**

Line a rimmed baking sheet with paper towels. Place a wire cooling rack on top of paper towels. Set aside.

FOR ONION RINGS: Separate onion into rings. In a large resealable plastic bag, combine onion and 2 tablespoons flour. Seal bag, and shake well. In a large bowl, combine remaining 1 cup flour, cornmeal, and ½ teaspoon salt. Add beer and hot sauce, whisking until combined.

In a large deep cast-iron skillet, pour oil to halfway full. Heat oil over medium-high heat until a deep-fry thermometer reads 350°. Working in batches, remove onion from bag, and dip in beer mixture, allowing excess to drip off. Carefully place onion in hot oil. Fry until golden brown, approximately 3 minutes, turning occasionally. (Adjust heat as needed to maintain 350°.) Using a slotted spoon, remove onion rings from oil; let drain on prepared pan. Sprinkle with remaining ½ teaspoon salt.

FOR SAUCE: In a medium bowl, stir together mustard, vinegar, and honey. Serve with onion rings.

Bacon-Balsamic Brussels Sprouts

YIELD: 4 TO 6 SERVINGS

4 slices thick-cut bacon, chopped
1 pound Brussels sprouts, ends trimmed and cut in half
½ cup chopped fresh parsley
¼ cup balsamic glaze
2 teaspoons lemon zest
1 teaspoon salt
1 teaspoon ground black pepper

Heat a large cast-iron skillet over medium heat. Add bacon, and cook until crisp, approximately 6 minutes. Remove with a slotted spoon, and let cool. Crumble, and set aside. Reserve rendered bacon fat in pan.

Add Brussels sprouts to pan, and cook until crisp and browned on the outside and tender throughout, approximately 10 minutes. Add parsley, balsamic glaze, lemon zest, salt, and pepper; stir to combine. Spinkle with bacon.

Potato-Apple Skillet Fries

YIELD: APPROXIMATELY 6 SERVINGS

4   **tablespoons canola oil**

2   **cups chopped yellow onion**

4   **cups chopped baking or russet potato**

½   **cup apple cider**

1½ **cups cored and chopped Granny Smith apple (about 1½ apples)**

1   **tablespoon roughly chopped fresh thyme**

1½ **teaspoons kosher salt**

⅛   **teaspoon ground black pepper**

In a large cast-iron skillet, heat canola oil over medium-high heat. Add onion; cook, stirring occasionally, until softened and golden brown, approximately 10 minutes. Add potato, and cook 2 minutes. Add cider; cover skillet, and cook until potato is tender, approximately 7 minutes.

Stir in apple, thyme, salt, and pepper. Cook until potato is crisp and apple is tender, approximately 5 minutes.

Grilled Cabbage Wedges

YIELD: APPROXIMATELY 6 SERVINGS

GRILLED CABBAGE

1   head red or green cabbage
     (We used half of each.)
1   tablespoon canola oil
1   teaspoon kosher salt
¼   teaspoon ground black pepper

SAUCE

1   cup sour cream
¼   teaspoon lime zest
1   tablespoon plus 1 teaspoon
     fresh lime juice
1   tablespoon water
¼   teaspoon smoked paprika
¼   teaspoon kosher salt
⅛   teaspoon ground red pepper

Heat a cast-iron grill pan over high heat.

FOR GRILLED CABBAGE: Slice cabbage in half, leaving core intact. Slice each half into 3 wedges. Brush wedges with canola oil; season with salt and pepper. When pan begins to smoke, add cabbage, cut side down.

Cook until cabbage begins to char and soften, approximately 6 minutes per side.

FOR SAUCE: In a small bowl, stir together sour cream, lime zest and juice, 1 tablespoon water, paprika, salt, and red pepper. Serve over wedges. Store, covered, in refrigerator up to 2 days.

Stove-Top Macaroni and Cheese

YIELD: APPROXIMATELY 6 SERVINGS

4   slices bacon, cut into ¼-inch
     pieces
2   tablespoons all-purpose flour
2   cups warm whole milk
½   teaspoon kosher salt
¼   teaspoon ground dry mustard
¼   teaspoon hot sauce
¼   teaspoon Worcestershire sauce
1½   cups shredded American cheese
1½   cups shredded sharp Cheddar
     cheese
1   tablespoon minced fresh chives
8   cups hot cooked elbow macaroni
     (about 3 cups uncooked)

In a 10-inch cast-iron skillet, cook bacon over medium heat until crisp, approximately 6 minutes. Remove bacon with a slotted spoon, and set aside. Reserve rendered bacon fat in pan.

Whisk flour into warm rendered bacon fat. Cook, whisking constantly, 2 minutes. Whisk in milk, salt, mustard, hot sauce, and Worcestershire. Bring to a simmer. Cook, whisking frequently, until thickened, approximately 15 minutes.

Remove from heat. Add cheeses, stirring until melted and mixture is smooth. Stir in bacon, chives, and cooked macaroni.

Crispy Root Vegetable Roast

YIELD: 6 TO 8 SERVINGS

5   tablespoons unsalted butter,
      melted and divided
2   baking or russet potatoes, peeled
2   sweet potatoes, peeled
1   rutabaga, peeled
1   turnip, peeled
6   cloves garlic, smashed
2   teaspoons kosher salt
½   teaspoon ground black pepper
Garnish: fresh thyme sprigs

Preheat oven to 400°. In a 12-inch cast-iron skillet, add 2 tablespoons melted butter, swirling to coat bottom.

Using a knife or mandoline, slice potatoes, rutabaga, and turnip into ⅛-inch-thick rounds. Keeping sliced vegetables together by type, place in skillet. Tuck in garlic among sliced vegetables. Brush vegetables with remaining 3 tablespoons butter; sprinkle with salt and pepper.

Bake until tender and golden brown, approximately 1 hour and 30 minutes. Garnish with thyme, if desired.

Sweets

Peach Cobbler

YIELD: APPROXIMATELY 6 SERVINGS

CRUST

- 1   **cup all-purpose flour**
- 2   **teaspoons sugar**
- ¼   **teaspoon salt**
- ¼   **cup cold butter,**
       cut into small pieces
- 1   **tablespoon all-vegetable**
       shortening
- 3   **to 4 tablespoons ice water**

COBBLER

- 5   **cups (¾-inch-thick) sliced**
       fresh peaches (about 6 medium
       peaches)
- ⅓   **cup firmly packed light brown**
       sugar
- 2   **tablespoons all-purpose flour**
- ½   **teaspoon ground cinnamon**
- ⅛   **teaspoon ground nutmeg**
- ⅛   **teaspoon salt**
- 2   **tablespoons unsalted butter,**
       cut into small pieces
- 2   **teaspoons fresh lemon juice**
- 1   **tablespoon heavy whipping cream**
- 2   **teaspoons sugar**

FOR CRUST: In the work bowl of a food processor, combine flour, sugar, and salt; pulse 3 times. Add butter and shortening; pulse until mixture resembles coarse crumbs, 4 to 6 times. Spoon mixture into a bowl; add ice water, 1 tablespoon at a time, tossing just until moistened. Press dough into a 5-inch disk; wrap with plastic wrap. Refrigerate 30 minutes.

On a lightly floured surface, roll dough into an 11-inch circle. Cut dough into 9 strips.

FOR COBBLER: Preheat oven to 375°.

In a 10-inch cast-iron skillet, toss together peaches, brown sugar, flour, cinnamon, nutmeg, and salt. Dot with butter, and sprinkle with lemon juice.

Place dough strips over filling in a lattice design, sealing at edges. Brush dough with cream, and sprinkle with sugar.

Bake until filling is bubbly and crust is lightly browned, approximately 35 minutes. Let cool on a wire rack 20 minutes before serving.

Warm Chocolate Lava Cakes

YIELD: 6 TO 8 SERVINGS

½ cup semisweet chocolate morsels

¼ cup heavy whipping cream

1 (18.3-ounce) package fudge brownie mix, such as Betty Crocker

Garnish: confectioners' sugar

In a small microwave-safe bowl, place chocolate and cream. Microwave in 30-second intervals until melted, stirring in between each interval. Refrigerate until firm, approximately 1 hour.

Preheat oven to 350°. Place a cast-iron mini cake pan or muffin pan in oven to preheat.

Prepare brownie mix according to package directions. Carefully remove pan from oven; spray with nonstick baking spray with flour. Fill wells halfway full with batter. Place 1 teaspoon chilled chocolate mixture in center of each batter-filled well; top evenly with remaining batter.

Bake until set, approximately 16 minutes. Let cakes cool in pan 2 minutes. Carefully invert cakes onto a wire rack. Garnish with confectioners' sugar, if desired. Serve warm.

Blueberry Crumb Skillet Cake

YIELD: 8 TO 10 SERVINGS

1⅓ cups plus 1¼ cups
   all-purpose flour, divided
1 cup sugar, divided
⅓ cup lightly packed light brown
   sugar
2 teaspoons dried lavender
1 teaspoon kosher salt, divided
½ cup unsalted butter, melted
6 tablespoons unsalted butter,
   softened
2 large eggs, at room temperature
1 large egg yolk, at room
   temperature
1 teaspoon vanilla extract
⅓ cup sour cream, at room
   temperature
⅓ cup vanilla-flavored yogurt,
   at room temperature
2 tablespoons honey
1 teaspoon baking powder
¼ teaspoon baking soda
2 cups fresh blueberries

Preheat oven to 350°.

In a medium bowl, combine 1⅓ cups flour, ¼ cup sugar, brown sugar, lavender, and ½ teaspoon salt. Stir in melted butter until well combined. (Mixture will be crumbly.) Set aside.

In a large bowl, combine softened butter and remaining ¾ cup sugar. Beat at medium speed with an electric mixer until fluffy, approximately 4 minutes. Add eggs and yolk, one at a time, beating well after each addition. Add vanilla, beating well. Scrape down sides of bowl. Add sour cream, yogurt, and honey, beating until well combined.

In a medium bowl, sift together remaining 1¼ cups flour, baking powder, baking soda, and remaining ½ teaspoon salt. With mixer on low speed, add flour mixture to butter mixture, beating just until combined.

Gently fold in blueberries. Pour batter into a 10-inch enamel-coated cast-iron skillet, smoothing top. Crumble topping evenly over batter.

Bake until a wooden pick inserted in center comes out clean, approximately 45 minutes. Let cool slightly before serving.

Skillet Blackberry Cobbler

YIELD: 10 TO 12 SERVINGS

6   cups fresh blackberries or
     3 (12-ounce) packages frozen
     blackberries
1   cup firmly packed light brown
     sugar
¼   cup fresh orange juice
1   tablespoon vanilla extract
½   teaspoon ground cardamom
¼   cup cornstarch
3   tablespoons water
1½   cups all-purpose flour
¼   cup sugar
1½   teaspoons baking powder
½   teaspoon salt
6   tablespoons chilled butter,
     cut into small pieces
½   cup heavy whipping cream
1   tablespoon sanding sugar

Preheat oven to 375°.

In a 10-inch cast-iron skillet, stir together blackberries, brown sugar, orange juice, vanilla, and cardamom over medium-high heat. Bring to a simmer, and cook until juice is released from blackberries and mixture is hot and bubbly, approximately 10 minutes.

In a small bowl, stir together cornstarch and 3 tablespoons water. Slowly add to berry mixture, stirring to combine. Cook until thickened, approximately 3 minutes. Remove from heat.

In a medium bowl, whisk together flour, sugar, baking powder, and salt. Add butter. Combine with fingertips until crumbly. Add cream, and stir gently until a biscuit-like dough forms.

Tear dough into 3-inch-round pieces; arrange over berries. Sprinkle dough with sanding sugar.

Bake until topping is lightly browned, approximately 30 minutes.

Chocolate Chip-Oatmeal-Peanut Butter Skillet Cookie

YIELD: APPROXIMATELY 4 SERVINGS

½ cup unsalted butter, softened

¾ cup firmly packed light brown sugar

1 large egg

1 teaspoon vanilla extract

¾ cup all-purpose flour

¾ teaspoon baking powder

¼ teaspoon kosher salt

¾ cup old-fashioned oats, divided

½ cup creamy peanut butter

⅓ cup semisweet chocolate morsels

Preheat oven to 325°. Spray a 7-inch cast-iron skillet with nonstick cooking spray. Set aside.

In a large bowl, beat butter and brown sugar at medium speed with an electric mixer until fluffy. Add egg and vanilla; beat until combined.

In a small bowl, whisk together flour, baking powder, and salt. Reduce mixer speed to low; add flour mixture to butter mixture, beating just until combined. Stir in ½ cup oats.

Press half of dough into bottom of skillet. Spread peanut butter evenly over dough. Drop spoonfuls of remaining dough over peanut butter. Sprinkle with chocolate and remaining ¼ cup oats.

Bake until golden brown, approximately 45 minutes. (Cover loosely with aluminum foil to prevent excess browning, if necessary.) Let cool 15 minutes.

Strawberry Pound Cake

YIELD: APPROXIMATELY 6 SERVINGS

½ cup butter, softened
½ cup sugar
1 large egg
2 tablespoons whole milk
1 teaspoon vanilla extract
1 cup all-purpose flour
8 ounces fresh strawberries, stems removed and halved (about 3 cups)

Preheat oven to 350°.

In a large bowl, beat butter and sugar at high speed with an electric mixer until creamy. Add egg, milk, and vanilla, beating until combined. Gradually add flour, beating just until combined. Pour batter into a 1-quart cast-iron oval baking dish. Arrange strawberries on top.

Bake until set and a wooden pick inserted in center comes out clean, approximately 30 minutes. Let cool 15 minutes before serving.

Caramel Apple Pie

YIELD: APPROXIMATELY 8 SERVINGS

FILLING

6   medium Granny Smith apples,
     peeled, cored, and cut into wedges
½   cup all-purpose flour
½   cup sugar

CARAMEL

1½ cups sugar
¼   cup water
1½ teaspoons fresh lemon juice
1   cup heavy whipping cream
2   tablespoons unsalted butter

½   (14.1-ounce) package
     refrigerated piecrusts (1 sheet)

Preheat oven to 350°.

FOR FILLING: In a medium bowl, toss apples with flour and sugar; set aside.

FOR CARAMEL: In a 10-inch cast-iron skillet, stir together sugar, ¼ cup water, and lemon juice over low heat until sugar dissolves. Increase heat to high; boil without stirring until mixture is deep amber in color, approximately 5 minutes. Remove from heat, and add cream. Return to low heat; stir until any bits of caramel dissolve. Add butter, whisking until smooth. Transfer to a medium bowl.

Add apples to skillet, and top with caramel sauce. Unroll piecrust, and cut into 9 strips. Place dough strips over filling in a lattice design, sealing at edges.

Bake until filling is bubbly and crust is golden, approximately 1 hour.

Chocolate Fudge Cake

YIELD: APPROXIMATELY 12 SERVINGS

½ cup hot water
3 ounces unsweetened chocolate, chopped
1 tablespoon instant coffee powder
½ cup unsalted butter, softened
2 cups sugar
2 large eggs
1 teaspoon vanilla extract
2 cups sifted cake flour
1 teaspoon baking soda
1 cup sour cream
8 ounces semisweet chocolate, chopped
½ cup heavy whipping cream

Preheat oven to 350°.

In a medium bowl, combine ½ cup hot water, unsweetened chocolate, and coffee. Stir until chocolate melts and coffee powder dissolves. Set aside.

In a large bowl, beat butter and sugar at high speed with an electric mixer until fluffy. Add eggs and vanilla, beating to combine. Add melted chocolate, stirring to combine. Add flour, baking soda, and sour cream; beat just until combined. Pour batter into a 12-inch cast-iron skillet.

In a microwave-safe bowl, place semisweet chocolate and cream. Microwave 1 minute. Let stand 5 minutes; whisk until smooth. Pour melted chocolate over batter, and swirl with the tip of a knife.

Bake until sides pull away from pan, approximately 30 minutes. Serve cake warm from skillet.

Orange Sweet Rolls

YIELD: APPROXIMATELY 8 SERVINGS

ROLLS

1	cup warm water (about 120°)
3½	cups all-purpose flour
6	tablespoons unsalted butter, melted
1	(¼-ounce) package active dry yeast
3	tablespoons sugar
2	teaspoons salt
¼	cup nonfat dry milk
2	tablespoons orange zest
½	cup orange marmalade
½	teaspoon ground ginger

ICING

4	ounces cream cheese, softened
4	tablespoons butter, softened
2	cups confectioners' sugar

FOR ROLLS: In a large bowl, combine 1 cup warm water, flour, melted butter, yeast, sugar, salt, dry milk, and orange zest. Beat at low speed with an electric mixer until combined. Place dough in a large bowl. Lightly spray top of dough with nonstick cooking spray, and cover. Let rise in a warm draft-free place until doubled in size, approximately 1 hour.

On a lightly floured surface, knead dough until smooth and elastic, 5 to 7 minutes. Roll dough into a 20x12-inch rectangle, approximately ¼ inch thick. In a small bowl, stir together marmalade and ginger. Spread mixture evenly over dough. Beginning on one long side, roll tightly into a log. Place log, seam side down, on a cutting board, and cut into 2-inch rolls.

Spray a 10-inch cast-iron skillet with nonstick cooking spray. Place rolls in pan; cover, and let rise in a warm draft-free place 1 hour.

Preheat oven to 350°. Bake until lightly browned, approximately 35 minutes.

FOR ICING: In the bowl of a stand mixer fitted with the whisk attachment, beat cream cheese and butter at medium speed until smooth. With mixer on low speed, add confectioners' sugar. Beat at high speed until fluffy. Spread icing over warm rolls.

Pineapple Upside Down Cake

YIELD: APPROXIMATELY 8 SERVINGS

TOPPING

¼	cup butter
½	cup sugar
2	tablespoons water
1	pineapple, peeled and cored

CAKE

2	cups cake flour
1	teaspoon baking powder
1	teaspoon salt
¾	cup whole milk
2	teaspoons vanilla extract
2	tablespoons spiced rum
6	tablespoons butter, softened
1½	cups firmly packed light brown sugar
2	large eggs

FOR TOPPING: Preheat oven to 350°.

In a 10-inch cast-iron skillet, melt butter over medium heat. Stir in sugar and 2 tablespoons water. Bring to a simmer; reduce heat to medium-low. Cook, stirring occasionally, until smooth, 3 to 5 minutes. Remove from heat, and let cool 10 minutes.

Cut pineapple into ¼-inch-thick slices; cut each slice into quarters. Arrange pineapple pieces in concentric circles over topping in skillet. Set aside.

FOR CAKE: In a medium bowl, whisk together flour, baking powder, and salt. Set aside. In another bowl, combine milk, vanilla, and rum. Set aside.

In a large bowl, beat butter and brown sugar at medium speed with an electric mixer until fluffy. Add eggs, beating to combine. With mixer on low speed, add flour mixture to butter mixture in thirds, alternating with milk mixture, beginning and ending with flour mixture. Beat until combined. Pour batter over pineapple in pan.

Bake until a wooden pick inserted in center comes out clean, approximately 1 hour. Let cake cool in pan 20 minutes before inverting onto a cake plate. Let cool before serving.

Grilled S'more Sandwiches

YIELD: 6 SERVINGS

6   tablespoons unsalted butter, softened

12   (½-inch-thick) slices bread, such as brioche

1   cup plus 2 tablespoons chocolate-hazelnut spread, such as Nutella

1   cup plus 2 tablespoons marshmallow crème, such as Marshmallow Fluff

1½   teaspoons kosher salt

Butter 1 side of each bread slice.

Preheat a cast-iron skillet over medium-high heat.

On unbuttered side of 1 bread slice, spread 3 tablespoons chocolate-hazelnut spread. On unbuttered side of another bread slice, spread 3 tablespoons marshmallow crème. Press slices together, buttered side out. Repeat with remaining bread, chocolate-hazelnut spread, and marshmallow crème.

Grill until golden brown and chocolate-hazelnut spread and marshmallow crème are melted, 3 minutes per side. Sprinkle each sandwich with ¼ teaspoon salt. Serve warm.

Strawberry Crisp

YIELD: APPROXIMATELY 6 SERVINGS

FILLING

5 **cups fresh strawberries,
stems removed and halved**
¼ **cup sugar**
2 **tablespoons cornstarch**
⅛ **teaspoon salt**
1 **tablespoon butter, cut into
small pieces**

TOPPING

¾ **cup quick-cooking oats
(not instant)**
⅓ **cup firmly packed light
brown sugar**
⅓ **cup whole-wheat flour**
⅓ **cup butter, softened**
¼ **teaspoon salt**
⅓ **cup chopped pecans**

Preheat oven to 350°.

FOR FILLING: In a large bowl, toss together strawberries, sugar, cornstarch, and salt. Spoon mixture into a 10-inch enamel-coated cast-iron skillet; top with butter.

FOR TOPPING: In a medium bowl, add oats, brown sugar, flour, butter, salt, and pecans. Combine with fingertips until crumbly. Sprinkle over strawberry mixture.

Bake until topping is lightly browned and filling is bubbly, 25 to 30 minutes. Let cool 10 minutes before serving.

Pecan Sticky Rolls

YIELD: 1 DOZEN ROLLS

DOUGH

3½ cups all-purpose flour, divided

1 (¼-ounce) package active dry yeast

½ cup whole milk

½ cup sour cream

⅓ cup butter, cubed

⅓ cup sugar

½ teaspoon salt

1 teaspoon vanilla extract

1 large egg, lightly beaten

FILLING

¼ cup butter, softened

¼ cup sugar

2 teaspoons ground cinnamon

1 teaspoon orange zest

1 teaspoon all-purpose flour

⅛ teaspoon salt

GLAZE

½ cup firmly packed light brown sugar

⅓ cup butter

⅓ cup light corn syrup

⅛ teaspoon salt

½ cup toasted pecans, chopped

FOR DOUGH: In a large bowl, combine 1½ cups flour and yeast. Set aside.

In a medium saucepan, combine milk, sour cream, butter, sugar, and salt. Cook over medium heat, stirring occasionally, until a candy thermometer reads 120° to 130°. Pour over flour mixture. Add vanilla and egg; stir well. Gradually stir in enough remaining flour until a soft dough forms and pulls away from sides of bowl (approximately 1½ cups).

On a lightly floured surface, knead dough until smooth and elastic, 5 to 7 minutes. (To keep dough from sticking, add remaining flour, 2 teaspoons at a time, as needed.) Place dough in a large bowl. Lightly spray top of dough with nonstick cooking spray, and cover. Let rise in a warm draft-free place (85°) until doubled in size, approximately 1 hour and 15 minutes.

Lightly punch dough down. Cover, and let stand 5 minutes. On a lightly floured surface, roll dough into a 14x10-inch rectangle.

FOR FILLING: Spread butter over dough. In a small bowl, stir together sugar, cinnamon, orange zest, flour, and salt. Sprinkle over butter; gently press mixture into dough. Starting with one long side, roll dough into a log; pinch seam to seal. Place log, seam side down, on a cutting board, and cut into 12 rolls. In a 10-inch cast-iron skillet, place rolls. Cover, and let rise in a warm draft-free place until doubled in size, approximately 45 minutes.

Preheat oven to 350°. Uncover rolls. Bake until golden brown, approximately 25 minutes. Let cool in pan on a wire rack 30 minutes.

FOR GLAZE: In a medium saucepan, combine brown sugar, butter, corn syrup, and salt. Bring to a boil over medium heat, stirring frequently. Cook 1 minute, stirring frequently. Stir in pecans, and let stand 3 minutes. Pour over rolls.

Coconut-Pecan Pie Wedges

YIELD: 8 SERVINGS

½ (14.1-ounce) package refrigerated piecrusts (1 sheet)

2 large eggs

½ cup firmly packed light brown sugar

⅓ cup light corn syrup

¼ cup unsalted butter, melted

½ teaspoon vanilla extract

½ teaspoon kosher salt

⅛ teaspoon ground cinnamon

1 cup chopped pecans

½ cup sweetened flaked coconut

Preheat oven to 350°.

On a lightly floured surface, roll piecrust into a 12-inch circle. Using a pizza cutter or knife, cut dough into 8 even triangles. Press triangles into bottom and up sides of a 9-inch cast-iron wedge pan. Crimp edges as desired.

In a medium bowl, stir together eggs, brown sugar, corn syrup, melted butter, vanilla, salt, and cinnamon until combined. Stir in pecans and coconut. Divide batter evenly among wedges.

Bake until crust is golden brown and centers are set, approximately 30 minutes. Let cool in pan 30 minutes. Serve warm or at room temperature.

Baked Caramel Apples

YIELD: 6 SERVINGS

6   Gala apples
4   ounces cream cheese, softened
¼   cup firmly packed light brown
     sugar
¼   cup prepared caramel sauce
¼   cup candied pecans, chopped
¼   cup chopped sugared dates
1   teaspoon apple pie spice
2   tablespoons butter, softened
     and divided
½   cup coarsely ground gingersnap
     cookies
Garnish: additional prepared
     caramel sauce

Preheat oven to 375°.

Slice ½ inch off tops of apples, including stems. Set tops aside. Remove cores to within ½ inch from bottoms of apples. (Make holes 2 inches wide.)

In the work bowl of a food processor, combine cream cheese, brown sugar, caramel sauce, pecans, dates, and apple pie spice. Pulse until combined. Fill each apple with approximately 2 tablespoons cream cheese mixture. Dot each apple with 1 teaspoon butter. Replace apple tops. Place apples in a cast-iron mini cake pan.

Bake until tender, approximately 25 minutes. Remove from oven. Remove apple tops. Sprinkle with gingersnap crumbs, and replace tops. Drizzle with caramel sauce just before serving, if desired. Serve immediately.

INDEX